The Winner School

Janet McGuirk

Published by

 Melrose Books

An Imprint of Melrose Press Limited
St Thomas Place, Ely
Cambridgeshire
CB7 4GG, UK
www.melrosebooks.co.uk

FIRST EDITION

Cover designed by Melrose Books

**ISBN   978-1-912333-36-3 Paperback
          978-1-912333-37-0 epub
          978-1-912333-38-7 mobi**

Printed and bound in Great Britain by:
Ashford Colour Press Ltd
Unit 600
Fareham Reach
Fareham Road
Gosport
PO13 0FW

Dedication

This book is dedicated to my husband, Peter, as he always said when we were in Khartoum that we should write a book when we returned. Peter said this was our last adventure, and unfortunately that is the way it turned out for him, but I wouldn't have missed the experience, and neither, I think, would he.

I remain indebted to all our students and friends who helped us in our time of need. You all know who you are.

Contents

Chapter 1

The Start of the Adventure

My story begins in Danbury in Essex where I had lived with my husband Peter and son Christopher for the past ten years. I was the director of a homestay organisation, and was arranging stays for foreign students to learn English when I was approached by a consultant who worked very closely with Sudan. He asked me if I would be prepared to arrange stays for Sudanese students. At that time I had many European students and some Far Eastern, and I didn't think it would be any more difficult to have Sudanese. How wrong could I have been. Because of the difficulties in obtaining visas, often they didn't arrive on the date they said they would, and, more importantly, as they often had to wait for a flight, and couldn't book it until they had a visa. The visa often didn't cover the duration of the stay. I became quite familiar with visits to the Home Office in Croydon.

The first student to arrive, Ahmed, was actually a personal assistant to a politician in Khartoum. He should have arrived in July, but actually arrived in October. The problem was that it was very difficult to obtain a visa to travel to England, and often they could be delayed months dependent on the political situation in Khartoum. Ahmed arrived very smartly dressed in a suit and tie, but no winter coat. The first stop had to be to purchase a coat for him as he was frozen. In Khartoum, the temperature very rarely dipped below fifty degrees even in the rainy season. He had some command of English and was very polite. One of my best memories of Ahmed was us taking him to London, and his wanting a picture of himself sat astride one of the lions in Trafalgar Square.

At this time I had David working with me. David was Hungarian, and I had taken him on to assist me with the business. David had come to England initially to work as an au pair with a family, but when I met David, unfortunately the father had lost his job. David had rented out his apartment and booked his flight before he received this information, so he decided to come to England anyway in the hope of finding employment. In the meantime I had this brainwave that I needed help, and why not employ an au pair and give a package including English tuition. I contacted an agency, but I wasn't sure if it would be allowed as I had no children at home; but they said it would be fine, and they had a Hungarian on their books at the moment, although he was male and some families wanted a girl. Of course, it didn't matter to me. As it happened, I had a meeting in London the following day so I arranged to meet David at Liverpool Street Station to interview him. When I met David he told me that he was sleeping on the couch of a friend, and illegally wiping the windows of cars in London. As a mother, my heart went out to him and I recruited him on the spot. A quick telephone call to Peter telling him I was bringing David home, and he was part of the family for two years. I still miss him today.

Anyway, I am going off the story. Ahmed felt that in Khartoum it was only men who had the important jobs, so he only spoke to David, and really ignored me in the beginning. When I told him that I was actually in charge he was quite shocked.

The most problematic student I had was Rehab. He arrived with another student, Akram, in mid-December. I went to collect them at the airport, and all I could see were two pairs of eyes as they were huddled in winter coats with their hoods pulled over their faces. The two students should have arrived in November and been back home for Christmas, but because of the delays with the visas they were late. I was dismayed to find that when I looked at the visas, there was only five days left on them. Akram told me that the immigration officer had told him that they would allow them through as they were being met by a language school, but they must go to immigration to extend the visa if they weren't to be viewed as illegal immigrants.

The following day I put them in my car, and drove the thirty miles to Croydon to the Home Office where the Immigration Department was based. The queue was enormous in the Office, and as many nationalities don't queue in their own country, many were what we would term 'jumping the queue'. One old African man was manhandled and told to go to the back of the queue by one of the security men. He didn't understand, and I felt very sad for him. It must be very frightening to leave your homeland and everything that is familiar to you, and arrive in this strange country. We were queuing, and a security guard walked up to Rehab and hissed at him, "Are you here for political asylum, because if so you are in the wrong queue." Rehab just looked very frightened. I said, "No, he is here to study, and I am here supporting him."

We waited in that queue over four hours, and I felt there must be a better system than this. Eventually we were ushered into an inner room, and questions were fired as to why they were in England. I was able to assist in the answering of the questions, and we must have satisfied them as we were then taken to another room where they asked us for proof of a bank account. In Khartoum, very few people have bank accounts as the currency is mainly cash, but without a bank account, apparently they couldn't extend the visa. At this point, Akram pulled out a bundle of notes to prove that he had enough money to support himself in England, and this, together with my showing the return flight tickets, seemed to appease the immigration officer.

I looked at my watch, and breathed a sigh of relief. We had been there for a total of eight hours, but thankfully the students could now stay for Christmas. However, the families that I had placed them with were not expecting them for Christmas. As you can appreciate, this is a special time in England, so I would now be hosting them for Christmas. The funniest incident which remains in my memory was on Christmas Day, and both Rehab and Akram were sat around the dining table with paper hats and whistles. Neither of them had experienced anything like the English Christmas, and they were spellbound. After about an hour of whistling, though, it did get a bit much. I remember both of them being fascinated by the tree, and wanting to switch the lights on and off. It was a tradition that I would put chocolate decorations on the tree for my son Christopher to find, and even though Christopher was grown now the tradition still lingered. The sight of two Sudanese men on their hands and knees by the tree looking for chocolate decorations will always remain with me.

After the Christmas festivities, Rehab and Akram were transferred to their host family homes, and certainly with Rehab the troubles began then. For breakfast in the morning, he insisted on having a concoction of Sugar Puffs and egg and jam on bread. He was having one-to-one tuition from his teacher in the morning, and in the afternoon he was free to go on excursions with the family to learn about the English way of life and culture. However, this wasn't what Rehab wanted to do, as after his lesson he just wanted to sleep. The family telephoned me as they received what we termed an Educational Visit Allowance, and they were conscious that they weren't doing this. I visited the family home, and Rehab was in bed so I called upstairs, "Come down, Rehab. I need to talk to you." He then shouted down, "I am in bed. You have to come to me." I told him that English ladies don't do that.

I had been accompanied by my Hungarian assistant David on this visit, and when Rehab came downstairs he talked to David and not myself as I was a woman. I told him that I was the boss, and that he needed to speak to me, not David. In Sudan, women are very rarely the boss, as I found when I later lived in Khartoum.

During Rehab's visit he was very high maintenance, as I found myself being called out to deal with problems virtually every day. The most difficult one was when he flooded the bathroom when cleansing himself for prayers; he forgot to switch the tap off, and unfortunately caused a major leak in the ceiling. Thankfully, the family had been with me for some time, and we worked together to deal with the situation. This particular family continued to work with me long after Rehab had returned to Khartoum.

Akram, however, was a joy to host as he wanted to experience everything about English life. I remember the family telephoning me one day to tell me that Akram had been in the fridge and found the bacon, and asked if he could have a sandwich. The family weren't sure how to tackle this, but I just said, "Tell him what it is." He also decided he wanted to continue studies in the UK, and not return to Sudan. I went to visit him and explained that if he didn't go back I wouldn't be able to obtain visas for future students, and they deserved their chance too. I told him that if he still wanted to do this, the best thing would be to go home and apply to attend a UK university. I said if he needed a letter of support I would be happy to provide one.

Even at the end of the stay we had problems as we all arrived at Heathrow airport and were told that because of bad weather the flight had been delayed until early the next morning. We decided to take Rehab and Akram on a trip to Brighton, which wasn't very far away, and we all spent a nice day on the beach and walking along the quaint streets. When we arrived back at the airport later that day we had to stay overnight waiting for the plane. I was always conscious that until the students went through check-in they were my responsibility so I waited too. Early the following morning they caught their plane, and I travelled home. I was asleep when I received a telephone call. Rehab had left his suitcase in Dubai as he had neglected to collect it for his connecting flight. Thankfully, I was able to deal with this, but they weren't easy students to host.

The one student who will always remain in my thoughts is Ghani. He was a journalist in Sudan, and the first time he came to England, I went to collect him at Heathrow. I waited a long time in the Arrivals hall, and there was no Ghani. I went to the information desk to see if there was a problem, and was told that he had forgotten to transfer his suitcase at Dubai, and they were having difficulty explaining to him that they would locate it and he would receive it in due course. They allowed me to go through to assist, and my first view of Ghani was him shouting in broken English asking where his suitcase was. I calmed him down and arranged for the suitcase to be delivered to me when found. Ghani was very cold as he just had a suit jacket on. He said, "We don't need coats in Sudan." I asked if there was one in his suitcase, but he said no, so we went shopping for a coat. No cheap coat for Ghani; he wanted a Burberry which was very expensive.

He stayed with us, and I remember taking him to London on an excursion. We were walking through Soho, and a scantily dressed prostitute beckoned my husband Peter over and asked if he would like some company. Ghani said, "Go, Mr Peter, go enjoy her, she look nice," but then followed this by saying in a matter-of-fact manner, "If you do this in Sudan you get stoned." The look on Peter's face— we didn't know whether to believe him or not. On one of his visits when he was staying with a family, they had to put child protection controls on the computer as he was accessing information which wasn't allowed.

One evening, I remember vividly as we received a telephone call at midnight, and it was Ghani asking the address of the family he was staying with. Apparently he was in a taxi rank, and couldn't understand that there was a queue and he needed to join it. He went to the front of the queue, but then couldn't remember the address. The taxi driver was getting quite irate and a few choice words were used. Christopher had answered the telephone, and he had to explain to the taxi driver where Ghani wanted to go, and then ask him to join the end of the queue.

I remember his second trip when he was travelling back to Sudan. He had decided he would go on a trip to London and his flight was early afternoon from Heathrow. He hadn't arrived back at the time that he stated, nor had he packed his suitcase. He was staying with one of my families and I received a frantic telephone call from them so I went to their home and packed Ghani's suitcase. It took quite a while to contact Ghani, but eventually I did and asked him to meet me at Ingatestone station and I would take him on to the airport. I remember vividly Ghani emptying his suitcase in the car park and putting numerous items in my boot, telling me that he would collect them at a later date. He still had too much luggage when we arrived at check-in so yet more was given to me. I kept those items for some considerable time.

I received a telephone call, if my memory serves me right, in February 2006. It was David, the same consultant who had made the initial introduction. He said that he was working with some business people who planned to open a language school in Khartoum, and they wondered whether I would consider travelling to Sudan and giving them some advice. It should be mentioned at this point that had the invitation come a few months earlier, as I would later find out had been on the cards, the outcome would have been very different. I probably would have gone on the initial visit, but not elected to move there. We had a pet dog—Flame, a Bedlington

Terrier—and while the whole family was attached to her, she was like my shadow, and I wouldn't have left her at home to undertake this project. I am sure anyone who keeps pets will sympathise with this. You can't just put your life down and up sticks when you have this commitment. However, Flame had fallen ill a few months earlier, and her discomfort was so pronounced that we had to have her put down.

More relevant at this point is the invitation itself. I was required to visit the Sudanese Embassy in London and obtain a visa, book a flight, and pack, with a view to getting there within two to three weeks. No mean feat, I am sure you will agree, but I set about preparing right away and as Peter was a little anxious about my travelling alone we obtained permission for my son Christopher to travel with me. It should be added that Christopher was a qualified teacher of English as a foreign language so would be extremely useful in the process. At the time of the visit he was on a break from university, so it had come at the right time.

Chapter 2

The First Visit

The visa for Sudan was processed relatively quickly, which surprised me as I felt it would be a highly complicated procedure. I remember listening to a Sandi Toksvig programme on the radio when she complained openly about how long it took for her to obtain a visa.

I remember my first sight of Sudan airport. Going through, I had to go into a small cubicle where a Sudanese woman, who was a customs official, searched me. I was to find that this was going to be a regular occurrence as I was a white woman, and it was very unusual to see one. For the first time, I experienced what it was like to be a minority. The baggage was just thrown on to a platform—no carousel like we find in England—so there was a fairly good chance that it would be damaged. At the time we arrived, there was a very important meeting of the Arab League in process, and all the hotels were booked up (allegedly).

As I walked through the arrivals hall I was to get my first glimpse of Mohammed. At that time I didn't know he would ultimately direct the school with myself. David, the consultant, and Ghani were with him. I felt reassured as there were two people who I knew. However, the first thing they told me was that all the hotels were booked because of the Arab League conference, and the only hotel with any rooms was the Hotel Sahara in Jamhoria Street, which is the main street in Khartoum. I later found out that our hosts deliberately didn't choose the best hotels as they wanted to see how we would cope in Sudan.

Although this was my first visit to the hotel, I would ultimately stay there on two occasions. Chris and I were given rooms at opposite ends of the corridor, which was a little disconcerting for me as I was in a strange country with nothing seeming familiar, and we had been separated to some extent. However, Chris didn't feel the same as he had studied Japanese at university, and had already spent a year in Japan. When I explored my room I was dismayed to find that there was a leak in the bathroom and water was pouring out. I was extremely worried that they would think I had damaged the room, and being unable to speak Arabic I wondered how I would explain.

Christopher came to make sure that I was okay and I explained the situation. We decided the best thing to do would be to tell reception of the problem and hope they understood. The first task was to find reception—no mean feat—but when we did, thankfully the receptionist spoke a little English and we were able to explain. I went back to the room, and about an hour later there was a knock at the door, and there was a Sudanese man stood there in the traditional clothing of a long white gown and sandals. He gestured to me that I should follow him. I had no idea where I was going, but didn't feel I had any option but to follow him. He took me to another room and asked if I liked it. At this point I realised that I was being given a change of room, and I smiled at him in acknowledgement. I collected my things and changed rooms.

As we weren't due to have a meeting until the following day, we decided we would have a walk to get our bearings. My first impression was how dusty and hot everywhere was, but, amazingly, although I suffer from asthma, it wasn't having an effect on me; indeed, I didn't suffer at all during my time in Khartoum.

Jamhoria Street was like an Aladdin's cave with many unusual shops, but no chemist, greengrocer or supermarket. You could buy anything: electronics, shoes, ivory and so much jewellery. In addition to the shops there were people sat in front of the shops selling goods on a piece of cloth. Whilst walking, I heard the term 'Khawaja' being shouted more than a few times. What I didn't know at that time was that this meant 'White person'. Many of them hadn't seen a white person as Khartoum isn't on the main tourist route. As time went on, I became very used to hearing this. What shocked me more than anything was the amount of these stallholders who were missing limbs. Living in England, and seeing what can be achieved with prosthetic limbs now, it seemed tragic so see people shuffling about on their bottoms for lack of health provision. During my time in Sudan I would witness this time and again. People didn't seem to have any consideration for their own safety; they would often walk into the road with cars coming, and hope that it would be okay.

Our meeting was the following day and we had been told that Mohammed would collect us from the hotel and take us to the meeting with the business people. However, the following morning I received a telephone call from Mohammed asking me to meet him at his shop, which was on Jamhoria Street a few blocks from the hotel. It turned out that Mohammed was a printer, and in fact he had met the consultant as he was also a writer and Mohammed had printed his books for him.

When we arrived, Mohammed explained that the people we were meeting were very busy, and we may have to wait some time before the meeting could take place. I was to find that this was always the case in Sudan We waited quite some time, and then Mohammed received a telephone call that they were now ready for us. We travelled just outside Khartoum and met the business people who were to be the backers for the language school. All were very enthusiastic and anxious to start the project, the reason being that a peace agreement had just been brokered and they felt this was the best time to see if it could succeed. It should be said that they had been trying to do this for twenty-five years, which is how long the civil war had lasted. It was decided we would come up with a rough plan of what we thought was needed in a language school. Christopher and I decided that what was needed was a state-of-the-art school whose building, if it didn't succeed, could be used for something else in the future. As Christopher was a teacher, we worked together to produce a layout with airy classrooms, a language lab, a library and hi-tech visual aids. In short, Khartoum would never have encountered anything like this.

Concerning the teachers, we also impressed on them the importance of hiring native speakers as foreign language teachers, largely due to the fact that the education system in Sudan had steered almost totally towards the Arabic language, and as a result the English teachers that Khartoum had were mainly Sudanese, whose second language was English and therefore they were not as effective as they might be. We left the meeting on the understanding that we would meet again the following day with our ideas.

The next day, at a loss as to what we would do whilst waiting for the call giving us the time for the meeting, I noticed that Christopher could do with a haircut, and a shave wouldn't go far wrong either. I asked Mohammed if there was a barber in the vicinity. He was happy to assist and introduced us to an Ethiopian barber who gave Christopher a buzz cut, and then proceeded to trim his beard with a cut-throat razor. Very Sweeney Todd, and I must admit I was a little nervous and thought: What have I done? However, the precision with which he wielded his blade was fascinating to watch and I don't think Christopher has been as clean shaven since.

We went back to the hotel and had our first taste of a shawarma, which is a wrap containing chicken and some variation of sour cream, and drank our first hibiscus drink, which apparently has many health benefits. Several hours later, we were summoned to the backers. We showed them the plans and they were making positive noises.

Feeling pleased we could be of assistance, we left thinking the trip had been very worthwhile. At this point I had no idea I was to be offered a position at the school, so this was purely a consultation as far as I was concerned.

With that, we flew home with lots of strange but true anecdotes of our short trip there. I knew I had a good relationship with my Sudanese contacts and was looking forward to welcoming more students in England, probably that summer.

I think you can imagine my surprise when, barely six weeks later, I received a telephone call to say that the backers had secured a villa on the prosperous Nile Street, overlooking the Nile, in the Garden City area, and that furnishing the school to our specifications was already underway.

Oh gosh, what had we started?

Chapter 3

What Will the Decision Be?

Peter, my husband, had been very successful in his career up to the point at which he enters this story. He had been a chief executive in the Magistrates Courts, had held management positions in local government finance departments, and at this stage was working as a consultant in a senior role with Transport for London. This contract, however, was due to end in September 2006, which was, conveniently, right at the time that these developments were taking place.

I was asked to make a second visit to Khartoum to see how the building was progressing. Bravely, in hindsight, I decided to visit alone this time. Peter was very anxious as it was quite a different matter to travel alone. However, the backers assured him that I would be met at the airport and taken good care of so he agreed, albeit a little reluctantly.

Upon arriving at Khartoum airport, I was whisked yet again into a dimly-lit cubicle to be searched. This second time it was scary as there was no one with me, and what if my escort just thought I had missed the plane and didn't check? With a sigh, I was allowed to proceed to baggage control and the arrivals point. Thankfully I could see Mohammed in the distance, waving to me.

I was taken to the Hotel Sahara again, which was a little strange as I asked if there was a conference on and was told no. The reason this time was that I was close to Mohammed's printing shop. The hotel reception greeted me like an old friend, and I was to find this time and again during my stay in Khartoum, that I would meet so many friendly people who would always be happy to assist if needed. My visit to the property on Nile Street was scheduled for the following day so that I could recover from my jet lag. The next morning I went into breakfast, and I wasn't very sure of the food which was being offered so I was eating very little. I looked up and there was a little crowd of waiters standing around making gestures that I should eat. I took my fork and started to eat what was on my plate and they all smiled and kept taking their fingers to their mouth to convince me to carry on eating. At that moment I realised that for all the negative press reports about Sudan, many of the people were lovely and very caring.

After breakfast I was summoned early to visit the school and I was extremely impressed. They had already done renovations and Mohammed was going to visit China to source desks, etc. As some countries had sanctions against Khartoum there were only certain countries which would trade with them, and one was China. I asked Mohammed if he had ever visited China before, and he said no, and he was a little apprehensive.

Later on, I had a meeting with the backers to advise them how I felt about what they had done with the building. I told them I was extremely impressed—and then they dropped their bombshell. The backers offered me a position as the director of the school, with Mohammed in place as the managing director, largely because they felt that at least one manager should speak Arabic and be male. I told them that I had my own business in the UK which I couldn't just leave, and I wouldn't be able to make a decision without speaking to my family. I was asked if I would think about it. I said I would, but didn't think it was a position I would be able to consider.

The following day I went home with the prospect of an awkward conversation with Peter on the cards. We discussed it at length, but didn't feel it was something we would consider as we had our home and life in England. Peter felt that it was a tremendous opportunity for me, and also for Christopher as he would gain valuable teaching experience, but he didn't feel it was for him and I wasn't going anywhere without him.

This was the decision I had come to when I received a further telephone call which complicated the matter further. The backers wanted me to visit for a third time, but this time bring Peter and then we could both see what they had managed to achieve. I felt sure they must have realised that I wasn't going anywhere without my family. Peter was happy to go, and we eventually settled on the beginning of July. On this visit they actually offered Peter a position as the director of a business school, but this never materialised. I think, in hindsight, that Peter was too well qualified, and they felt threatened.

When we arrived in Khartoum we were taken to the school, and they had kitted out an apartment to show us that it could be comfortable. We had a very spacious double bedroom with a bed, wardrobe and chest of drawers, and a sitting room with a sofa and two easy chairs. The bathroom had a bath, sink and toilet, but no shower, just a pipe; but to all intents and purposes they were putting every effort in to make us see that it could be okay living there. In addition there were three spare bedrooms which still needed furniture: one for Christopher, and two spares for when teachers arrived. On this visit we actually stayed in the apartment and not at the Hotel Sahara.

At this juncture we had still not decided whether any of us would go and live there. Christopher was apprehensive as he had finished university and was having difficulty finding employment, but didn't know whether if he went to Sudan he would be able to obtain employment in the UK afterwards. From Peter's point of view, he didn't know how his skill set would fit. He came round eventually, deciding that his consultancy contract was due to come to an end, and maybe we could give it a go to see how it panned out. If not, we could always return to the UK and Peter take up his consultancy again. If I am honest, I felt we would probably last a few months as the situation there was so volatile, and together with the desert and extreme heat never did I think we would last two years. With this in mind we decided to rent out our house in Essex on a short-term basis, and then if the worst happened we could come home.

As I didn't feel this was to be long term, thankfully I had an assistant who had helped me out on a casual basis, and she was prepared to hold the fort and run my company in England for me whilst I was away. She would also assist with anything I might need to be forwarded to Sudan, e.g. stationery. Without this support Sudan would not have been possible.

Once the decision had been made, the next hurdle was to tell family. My mother and myself had always had a difficult relationship as I think she felt that many of my ideas were often a little crazy and I hadn't thought them through properly. When I told her that the whole family was going to live in Sudan, and in a very short space of time, she countered with "Are you crazy?" I can perfectly understand what a shock it must have been for her; however, she knew that once I had made my mind up it was very likely to happen. Looking back, maybe she had a very valid point. My father, on the other hand—once he had recovered from the shock—told me it would be an adventure, but made me promise to be careful. He had done his national service in Malaysia and had always wanted to return, but never managed it.

Having discussed the matter with family, my next hurdle was to source the teachers, and this wasn't going to be an easy task. How many teachers would want to move to a country which had been in the grip of a civil war for twenty-five years? I was beginning to wonder if I was a little mad. However, I managed to source a group of teachers who were very different. All of them had a background of living in third world countries or an interest in learning more about them. The criteria for these teachers was that they had to be native English speakers, and qualified to teach English as a foreign language, having taken an accredited course.

As time went on, it became more apparent to me that often these teachers had a hidden agenda. Some were positive, and they wanted to learn more about Arabic culture for career experience, but others were less positive and more political. I soon realised that I had to be extremely careful with the teachers I was recruiting and needed to be aware of any political leanings. I had one who wanted to make a stand for human rights, and was even taking issue with the political views of the government of Sudan; and another who wanted to help their partner to escape over the border from Eritrea.

I learnt very quickly that what I proposed to do was very difficult if not nigh on impossible. I managed to recruit my first group of teachers and they were due to arrive in September so that I had time to prepare the school for them. I was very conscious that this was a third world country and, as such, the medical facilities, etc., were not likely to be of the same standard as the UK so I negotiated with the board that every teacher would have full medical insurance with BUPA, which included repatriation, and all their inoculations would be paid for as part of their package. I was conscious that it had to be excellent to tempt them to come. By the time all the references and plane tickets had been paid for, it was time for Christopher and I to travel to make our new life in Sudan.

Chapter 4

Our New Life Begins

On our arrival in Sudan—unfortunately without Peter, who was renting out our house and finishing his contract with Transport for London—we were met at the airport by Mohammed, and taken to the school. I was very dismayed when I arrived at the school to find that it was very dirty, and Mohammed told me that they had had squatters in the building. I couldn't believe that they had left it in this state, but as I was to learn over time, there is a phrase in Sudan—'Inshallah'—which means 'Not today, maybe tomorrow, or sometime in the future'. It wasn't unusual for them to promise something, and then you would wait for an indefinite period for it to happen

My first reaction was shock. What on earth had I signed up to? However, there was no way I had travelled halfway across the world and disrupted my family to give up now. I had a manager, a driver, and a caretaker as staff, and I asked them to get me cleaning materials as the school needed to be thoroughly cleaned. Once they had found the relevant materials, despite suffering from jet lag, I rolled up my sleeves preparing to clean the school. I asked the manager and driver to help and they told me that their job was not to clean the school. I asked them who was in charge of the school and they said, "You, as the director!" I said, "In that case we need to clean this school if we are to open next week." My son just stood there with his mouth open as he had never seen me speak that way. The manager dared to say, "You are the director and cannot clean the school," but I said, "I shall be cleaning it, and so will you." I think this was the first time a woman had told them what to do, but I found during my time there that because I was a white woman, I could get away with many things. It took quite a long time to get the school in some sort of shape, but it looked very clean once we had finished. I was extremely tired as I felt very jet-lagged.

At this point, the cleaner had not been recruited. Our first one was Sudanese and he was an excellent cleaner. I was very conscious that the school had to be professional and part of that was that it needed to be pristine. Each morning I would rise and go downstairs to the school and tell the cleaner what was required. He never spoke in English, but I very quickly realised that he did understand what I was saying to him. I asked him if he understood me and he just nodded his head. I later found that he couldn't admit to being able to speak English as he came from South Sudan and he would be unable to find a job. He told me that he had been taught by a local missionary and I think he would probably have been seen as a threat. I used to give him books to read and I promised I wouldn't tell anyone. Unfortunately, he left very suddenly to go to a new job, and I really was quite disappointed as I felt I had tried to help him.

We then recruited another cleaner who came from Bangladesh. He was totally different. I had to watch him all the time to make sure he was doing the job properly. He was what we would term in England a lovable rogue. He was only to work for one employer under the terms of his visa, but one day he was late for cleaning and I was to find he was working at another company. How I managed to keep him from being deported I don't know, but I did. I remember one conversation with him when he said, "If you take me to England with you when you return, I will clean your house for free for one year." He called me 'Auntie' and this was a great source of amusement to everyone, but I think he recognised I did try to help him. He told me that all his wage had to be returned to Bangladesh as otherwise his family wouldn't eat.

When Peter telephoned early into my arrival to ask how it was going, I knew I couldn't tell him the state the school was in when I arrived as he was giving up a lot to give me an opportunity of a lifetime. If we could make a difference it would be quite an achievement, but at this point I didn't know whether we could.

Whilst we were waiting for the teachers to arrive, I busied myself familiarising myself with the culture and making sure that the school was satisfactory. I quickly learnt that this was going to be very difficult as all the things I had taken for granted in England just weren't there. My oven in the communal kitchen (I didn't have one of my own in the apartment) was powered by Calor gas and I was told that if I ran out I would have to drive to the nearest petrol station to obtain another cylinder. It was often the case that I would run out halfway through cooking and have to get another one. I had a refrigerator, but no freezer. I fast became used to having a cold shower in the morning, and even when I was in our apartment I was constantly interrupted by people just walking in; there didn't seem to be any privacy. Any food I placed in the fridge or cupboards could disappear as the students felt that everything was to share. My main difficulty was finding food to eat and certainly, initially, I lived mainly off peanuts and mangoes, which obviously couldn't have been sustained. When Sarah, one of the teachers, arrived she was vegetarian so I added lentils to my diet, but I very quickly got fed up with the bland taste. As time went on I discovered different vegetables and even some meats. I quickly learnt that as they didn't use pesticides, the outer skin of these looked very unappetising, but they actually tasted quite good—but you had to obtain them as fresh as possible.

Each day I asked whether they could tell me how many students would be arriving on the opening day, and Mohammed just kept saying "They will arrive." Two days before the teachers were to arrive, I was becoming worried that we wouldn't have any students to teach so I asked again and said, "I need an answer now because if the teachers arrive and there are no students, how are we going to pay them?" I think Mohammed realised that I wasn't going to let it drop and said, "They will come in due course, Inshallah." I was so angry, I gestured to our driver Ahmed that he should come with me and walked towards the door of the school. Mohammed said, "Where are you going?" and I replied, "To find some students." I told Ahmed to drive, and I looked for buildings that might be companies; no mean feat, as often they were little more than large shacks with lettering above. It should also be noted at this point that there were no telephone directories or maps, and often no street names.

Eventually, we happened on what I thought might be a company. I can remember I was shaking so much with fear and nerves. I was an English woman not speaking a word of Arabic and I was about to walk into a company in another country without an appointment, trying to obtain business. Was I mad? However, I took a deep breath and walked in. There was a receptionist on the desk and she looked shocked to see a white woman in front of her. I asked if she understood English and she said a little, but walked away. I didn't know where she was going, but she came back with a man in tow who said he was the person in charge and what did I want? I told him that I had just moved to Sudan and was the director of a language school. I wondered if his staff needed to learn English. I think he was a little shocked to find me standing there, but he ushered me into his office. I had already decided that the way forward, and a future unique selling point, would be to design courses for their business needs, so I asked him what his staff needed and he told me that they needed help with communication by telephone, letter or email. I told him that we could design this and then our fully qualified native English speakers could teach the course. He seemed quite impressed with this so I told him I would visit the following day with a proposal and price.

When I arrived back at the school I asked Christopher to work on a course that I could present the following day, and I concentrated on pricing. I think Christopher was quite shocked that his mum had done this, but I was rapidly beginning to realise that I would have to think on my feet and not accept that anything was impossible if we were to succeed. This was the beginning of the 'crazy woman' as I became known.

I spoke to Mohammed when I arrived back at the school and told him what I had done. He was shocked that I had the courage to do this, but he said I was a miracle worker and this title stayed throughout my time in Khartoum. If work was thin on the ground Mohammed used to say 'Work a miracle'. The following day, prices had been worked out and agreed with Mohammed, which wasn't an easy task. I was to find, over time, that Mohammed ran his own printing business on the premise that they would all be one-offs, and therefore he charged accordingly. Throughout the time I was there I never managed to get him to grasp the concept of pricing in order to secure repeat business, which was the way I had always worked in England.

I set off to my meeting feeling a little more confident now as I had calculated a fair price for twelve sessions and felt, with any luck, I would manage to secure our first contract. Christopher had done an excellent job of working out what would be needed to improve their communication. When I arrived I was ushered into the same office as the day before and told to wait. Over time I was to realise that in Sudan the longer you had to wait, the more you were respected. That day I waited almost an hour and I was becoming so extremely nervous about that meeting, I didn't have any nails left. However, the manager eventually arrived and I showed him the course format and the pricing structure, which he seemed very impressed with. I later found that after that day the title 'crazy woman' evolved, as he told all his associates about this strange woman who had appeared, but nevertheless our first contract had materialised.

The following day I was collecting the first batch of teachers, whom I had already interviewed in England, from the airport. I can remember breathing a sigh of relief as I had been so worried that there would be no work for them. I wondered what they would make of Sudan and, more importantly, would they stay, or indeed would we be able to get this undertaking off the ground. If the Peace Agreement didn't hold we could all be on our way back to the UK within a matter of days or weeks. What on earth had I let myself in for? I remember the first three teachers coming through the barrier, and wondered if they were having the same thoughts as myself, but I was determined to give it a go. All the teachers were staying in the school initially so that they could become familiar with culture, etc,, but we had rented an apartment for them a short distance away, which they would move into when they were comfortable with their surroundings.

I visited the market in Khartoum, which was very different from English markets as you did not know what you would be able to buy. No stalls specialised in a specific product; they just seemed to have an abundance of everything. I was transfixed walking round, and it took me quite some time to understand the system of paying. There was no set price. You had to negotiate. Christopher was extremely good at this and obtained some excellent bargains, so I used to ask him to come with me. The strangest thing I saw was that the seamstresses were all men and I would have to visit them a few times as I needed clothing. I was very restricted as I wasn't allowed to show my arms, my tops had to come up to my neck, and I had to wear long skirts. I wasn't allowed to wear trousers. I remember one incident when I needed a new bra as I had lost rather a lot of weight, and my secretary took me to the market and to a man who would measure me, but I said 'no thanks' and went back to the school and measured myself. I asked my mother to send me some. There were numerous incidents like this.

I think the strangest experience for me was the first time I went to a hairdresser's as it was nothing more than a hut. I walked in and there were several Sudanese women sat on chaises longues, talking. Everyone pointed at me and said, "Khawaja." I wanted to run out of the door as I found it very intimidating. I was told to sit down, and I think because the hairdresser was so surprised to see me she did me next. I wasn't sure how I would ask how much it would cost so I gestured with the palm of my hand and she put 4 fingers up to tell me how much, which was the equivalent of about £1.50 in English currency. I was ushered to a chair with a bucket and pipe behind me and this was my first experience of having my hair washed with soap Sudanese style. I was a little anxious as I didn't know what my hair would look like at the end of this experience, but she did an excellent job. I noticed that on another chair a woman was having the hair removed from her face, but it was being done by a razor on a piece of string. I was fascinated with this and wondered whether I would be brave enough to have it done, but I reasoned whilst I was living there I should experience as much as I could. I asked if I could have the same treatment. I was a little scared as it was very different from electrolysis, but they too did an excellent job.

In time I found a Filipino hairdresser who told me that she had been in Sudan for several years and hadn't seen her daughter for ten years. She had started out on her journey hoping to come to England eventually, but Sudan was as far as she had travelled. However, she was very proud of her daughter who was a teenager now and doing very well at school. She said it was too late for her now, but she hoped that her daughter would have a better life. Her one wish was to see her daughter one more time. I hope she does.

Chapter 5

Teachers Arrival and School Open Day

The teachers having effectively recovered from their jet lag, it was now the opening day, and I was hoping and praying that the Communications course would arrive; but at the most this would occupy two teachers. What about the rest? Mohammed arrived with the news that he had managed to secure some local government officials to the tune of four classes and they would be commencing their course the following day. This would last for three months. As I now had two courses with the communications course, this meant that we would be able to pay the teachers initially. In addition to this I had random people arriving at the school as they had heard of the crazy English woman, and were curious to meet her. Many of these random callers signed up for individual tuition, which helped the coffers immensely. During my time there I often received cheques made out to 'Mrs Winner', and I was amazed that the bank always cashed them.

I would have some breathing space to secure new clients. I knew that this first day would be difficult, as all new enterprises are, but at this point I had absolutely no idea what I had let myself in for. The first task was to carry out a test to ascertain the English levels, and then I would hopefully be able to separate them into classes. I was pleasantly surprised to find that many of them had the basics of English, and some were very good as they had studied in English at their various universities. I didn't know until they turned up at the school how many students I would have, but on the second day I had approximately 100 students and thankfully all the teachers were prepared. We had managed to acquire whiteboards for every classroom, and I had brought marker pens from England as they were impossible to find in Khartoum. However, due to the heat they became dry very quickly and didn't work, so I needed a very large supply. I wrote to my assistant in England and asked her to send these immediately. However, it took three months for them to arrive, and then the package had been opened for security purposes and some were missing. I remember the first time I visited the building which held the post (not a post office as in England). I was shown to what resembled a factory floor with shelves up to the ceiling, and ladders. The shelves were numbered as to whose post it was. It was never delivered: you had to collect. I had to climb up a ladder to our shelf, and whilst I was doing this there were shouts of 'Khawaja'. It was quite disconcerting. Throughout my time in Khartoum, I found that often my and the teachers' packages had been opened and sometimes items were missing. In hindsight, maybe they thought 'khawajas' were spies.

What hadn't been explained to me was that, in Ramadan, often students would fall asleep at their desks as they had been awake early to pray and had not eaten, or would not turn up at all. As you can imagine, from my point of view it was extremely difficult to schedule the teachers, and then often the students would want to extend their classes to include the ones missed. Because of this, the funds to run the school were often very hit and miss. I often didn't pay myself so that the teachers would be paid and they would have their healthcare. I was always very conscious that we were in a Third World country, and an emergency could happen at any time.

My typical day commenced at 4 a.m. as my first job of the day was to supervise the cleaner: if we were to be professional, the school needed to be pristine. The prayers at the mosque, which was very near to the school, tended to start at 4a.m. I remember waking up on my first morning and feeling totally disorientated as I had never heard this before and wondered where I was for a moment. I would awaken early every day, and at times it was like living in a goldfish bowl as anyone could walk in at any time. I used to try and carry out my marketing duties between prayers and breakfast, which gave me a window of about four hours.

The classes started early, but this could be tricky as often the teachers would be on split shifts, and our contracts could vary. Most classes only continued for a few hours as the students had to return to their employment so we had to be extremely flexible. In Khartoum they have a saying 'Inshallah' which loosely means 'if God wills it'. I was to find very quickly that, in Sudan, the later a person is, the more they respect you. In the case of Khartoum it would often take months to get a firm answer from companies with regard to obtaining contracts.

Ahmed and I used to get in the minibus and drive, searching for companies to approach. This is hard to do in a city with no road maps and no street names. So instructions used to often involve 'the second donkey cart to the right' or 'the bread seller next to Jamhoria Street'. This of course poses the question—how do you find clients? Simple! You look at the beautiful green and white gates and the Arabic lettering on the sign, and walk in the front door. During my time I never made an appointment, just arrived. However, just before I left they were trying to complete a telephone directory. No mean feat as everything was done by way of mobile telephones.

Ahmed, my driver, was a lovely young man, and as you took your life in your hands to cross any road in Khartoum, he used to assist me across. Having negotiated the usual dice with death, I proceeded to walk into these companies and say, "Excuse me, I'd like to speak to the chief." Inevitably, the receptionist was so shocked to see me there that she would often interrupt meetings to get me in.

I should explain at this point that two things were unusual about me visiting. First, as I said earlier, I was a 'khawaja', a white person—but it should be added that this is a complimentary term in the Arab world. Second, I was a white woman sporting none of the traditional Islamic attire for women (in Sudan, local women are expected to wear the hijab—a scarf—around their heads to cover their hair). It is considered extremely uncouth for a woman to summon a director out of a meeting, khawaja or otherwise. However, during my time there I was amazed at how much I was allowed to get away with. Maybe because they called me the crazy woman they just accepted me.

Chapter 6

Ghani's Arrival

Shortly after the teachers arrived, I received a telephone call from Ghani. He wanted to take me on an outing on a boat on the Nile. (What should be mentioned at this time was that we were expecting the rainy season.) I waited all day, but there was no sign of Ghani, so Christopher decided to go for a walk. Just after he had left, I received a telephone call from Ghani saying he was on his way.

Sarah was in the school with me, and I asked her if she would like to join us as I knew Ghani wouldn't mind. Sarah was happy to come, and Ghani arrived and drove us to the Nile where there was a big old boat and lots of people waving at us. It turned out that Ghani had arranged an English tea party in my honour, and Akram was in attendance too. I remember it vividly as I was introduced to everyone, and they were all wanting to practise their English. The rains started, and it was a little turbulent on the Nile, but Ghani said, "No problem; it will be okay." However, once we had completed our sail, it was another matter to climb off the boat as all we had was a plank which was very wet. Both Ghani and Akram had to help both myself and Sarah off.

Ghani then drove us back to the school, and we both commented that we had never seen rain like it. When we arrived back at the school the water was coming in as none of the doors fitted very well, and we had to move the computers to a higher place to avoid them being damaged. It was then all hands on deck to brush the water out of the school. The Sudanese staff said that this was a normal occurrence each year.

I felt that that there must be something that we could do, and I had the brainwave to have bolsters which we had in the UK to stop draughts. I thought that they might stop some of the water. However, going to the market and trying to explain what I wanted was another matter, but eventually I managed to acquire them and they did make a slight difference.

Chapter 7

Al Fatih

One of the more unusual things I experienced was a visit to the 'whirling dervishes' (or Sufis). The teachers had every Friday off as this was a holy day. On their first Friday off I wanted to take them somewhere to show them the culture of the country. We hired a tuk-tuk, which is their definition of a taxi, and drove to Omdurman where the ceremony took place. What we didn't know was that as this was a Friday, it would be very difficult to find a tuk-tuk to bring us back to the school.

Sufis are probably best described as Islamic wise men. They are dressed in the traditional white gowns, and barefooted. They work themselves up into a frenzy chanting, and everyone just stands and experiences their traditional dance which plays a powerful role in Sudanese culture, both as a typically Sudanese tradition and as a religious ritual. This can go on for hours. For most people outside Sudan, this is an exciting spectacle to behold, and the teachers and I were very happy to have experienced it, but didn't really understand it.

When it was time to travel back, we were dismayed to find that we couldn't find transport, and we had no idea where we were as we had just asked the driver to take us to the whirling dervishes. In hindsight we should have asked him to wait. The only option we had was to start walking and hope that we reached the main road. After a good hour of walking, we heard a loud honking horn. A large pickup truck stopped next to us, and the driver said in English, "Excuse me, madam. You don't look like the usual chocolate people we get in our crowd. Can I take you where you want to go?"

I should stress at this stage that the man in question was African himself, hence why we can, to an extent, get away with repeating what he said. His name was Al Fatih, and he was a member of the Sufis who had just performed. Granted, in England, if a stranger offers you a lift, accepting it might be a bad idea. On the other hand, it isn't realistic to adopt the same principles in Sudan that you would in England. People have limited resources and on that basis, people tend to be more willing to help. It's a principle of sharing what you have.

Al Fatih suggested that the teachers sat in the back of the truck. Before they did that, however, he declared in his booming voice (he could roll an 'r' for hours if you let him) "Which of this magnificent company is in charge?" Sarah, in the spirit of this very theatrical introduction, declared that I was, to which he replied, "Hazaah! British, and a woman. We have Queen Victoria in our midst! My lady, you will sit in the front." He then proceeded to put a fancy cushion on the seat for comfort; to be honest, I felt like Queen Victoria. I would have quite liked to do the wave our Queen does where she spins her hand around at passers-by.

Being more than a little uneasy about getting in the front of this truck with this stranger, I resolved to do so anyway as we were running out of options. My husband Peter had not arrived yet, so the rather useful thing of having a designated driver on the weekend was not there. I dreaded to think what he would have made of this, though. He tended to take a dim view of impulsiveness on this scale.

We broke up the journey three times. Once was on the Omdurman Bridge to admire the Nile confluence (where the Blue and White Niles meet), and at this point we got a clear sense of Al Fatih's importance in the community. Normally you aren't allowed to stop on this bridge for security purposes, but we were surprised to note that policemen stopped to speak to him, and some even waved. We were introduced to several people walking on the bridge.

Many contacts were made on that bridge, and would later form a noticeable part of our client base. I suspect that was networking Sudanese style, and it tells us a lot about how dependent we have become on social networking as we have to use email, but they just cause a roadblock on a bridge

Secondly, we stopped at the home of one of Al Fatih's friends, Hassan, who was a respected sheikh within the Sufis, and as such commanded a similar level of esteem to Al Fatih. He took a shine to one of our teachers, but that is another story entirely. We drank mint tea, and chatted about Sufism. Al Fatih told Christopher he looked like a blacksmith (don't ask me the rationale in that. I think it was the black baggy T-shirt he was wearing); and we heard some of his father's poetry. Al Fatih's father was from Libya and a famous pacifist poet, who, by the sound of it, had a prominent position in popular culture

After an intriguing discussion, we got back in the pickup truck, and the teachers prepared to hang on for dear life once more. The speeches about Queen Victoria continued, and the track on the tape player was now 'Redemption Song' by Bob Marley. I can honestly say that was the first, but not the last, time I was serenaded by a dreadlocked, free-spirited whirling dervish. As we were driving, he stopped the truck suddenly and said, "I screaming, I screaming, you is screaming, we must all go for the ice cream, yes!" With that, he dived into the nearest shop, which was still open at 9 p.m. (trust me, Al Fatih never just walked; he preferred the grand entrance), and came out producing plastic bags with melting ice cream inside (you must remember it was very hot). We all tried to eat this ice cream, which, while delicious, was really impractical when you were tearing down an autoroute on a pickup truck. All I could think of at this point was that we didn't have a washing machine, and where was the nearest laundry?

We arrived home about 10 p.m. that night, and absolutely exhausted. I just fell into bed. However, the experience wasn't over as the following morning I was in my office, and I heard a big booming voice ask Nagla, my secretary, where Queen Victoria was. Al Fatih had arrived. What I thought had been a chance meeting would quickly turn into a friendship. Nagla was shocked, and said, "Do you know who that man is? He never just visits people." I just said, "He is visiting Queen Victoria" to which she replied, "But isn't your Queen called Elizabeth?" She was always slightly slow on the uptake where jokes were concerned.

Al Fatih explained that he had come to have a tour of the school, so I showed him the classrooms and computer room, which he seemed very impressed with. He told me that he wanted to take me on a visit to be introduced to his mother, who was an academic, apparently. She had expressed an interest in what we were trying to do. Unfortunately, she wasn't at the school, but I would have loved to have been introduced to her.

As a result of this encounter, clients who visited would have invariably heard about me, and tended to make a beeline for the boss lady, 'Mrs Winner', or—and we did hear this from some of our prospective students, who I assume knew Al Fatih—'The Queen'.

'Mrs Winner' had been engendered, but now, looking back on how it started, did I get demoted somewhere down the line from Queen Victoria?

Chapter 8

Tradesmen?

In England, if we had a problem such as a tile falling off the roof or a leak in the bathroom, it could be sorted very quickly. Shortly after I arrived in Khartoum there was such a leak in the bathroom. The school had to be designed to accommodate the beliefs of the students, and before prayers they had to be thoroughly clean. The bathrooms, as far as possible, were designed as an English bathroom with a shower and a toilet. One of the students had forgotten to turn off the shower nozzle and caused a leak. I asked if they could ring a plumber and they did, but three weeks later the leak was getting worse and no sign of the plumber. I asked them to chase it, and they came back saying 'Inshallah' which of course meant maybe tomorrow, next week, or in six months' time. I was learning that nothing was ever repaired quickly.

The first Christmas we were in Khartoum, I had done my best to make it as Christmassy as possible for the teachers and Peter and Christopher. One of our board had actually found us a Christmas tree, and I had tasked the students to help me make decorations. I still remember the looks on their faces once we had put decorations on the tree as many of them hadn't seen anything like this. Everyone took photographs, but it was so funny watching grown adults making decorations and enjoying it so much. Whilst I was there we celebrated both Eid and Christmas which was a lovely experience for both us and our students.

On Christmas Day I decided I would try and cook a nice meal with the ingredients I had to hand—no mean feat. No turkey or Christmas pudding for us, and certainly no brandy sauce. I put the cooker on, and halfway through I ran out of gas, which was the normal in Khartoum so we had to hop in the car and obtain a replacement. Luckily, it wasn't too far, and the meal was okay, albeit a little late. We sat in our little apartment watching *House* as this became one of Peter's favourite programmes. We had managed to obtain a pirate Sky system, but we were limited as to which programmes we could find. One which we watched regularly was *MasterChef*, and Christopher and I still watch this today. About halfway through the programme there was an almighty crash. We all ran downstairs to see what it was. The kitchen walls were tiled, and all the tiles had fallen off the wall. Many of them were broken when we looked. I don't know what they had stuck them on with; it certainly wasn't glue. It took three months for this to be repaired.

Christopher remembers a day when we had a workman working outside, and I walked calmly into the school and said to Peter, "Can you give me some money, only the workman has been bitten by a scorpion and we need to get him to hospital quickly for the antidote. He only has thirty minutes." Peter looked at me amazed, wondering why I wasn't panicking, but I had grown used to there being an emergency virtually every day and nothing fazed me at this point.

The school had installed air conditioning, I think, because they felt we wouldn't be able to cope with the heat which was regularly fifty degrees; and when this worked it was brilliant, but often it broke down and then came the wait for it to be repaired, which was often very long.

Now I am back in England I really appreciate our tradesmen, and if they are a day late, so what? We are very lucky where we live.

Chapter 9

Waiting for Peter to Arrive

Christopher and I arrived in August, but Peter's contract with Transport for London was not to finish until October when he would join us in Khartoum. We had brought mosquito nets as, although we had been inoculated against virtually everything, we were still a little wary of mosquitos. I had to take malaria tablets every day for the two years I was there. However, the air conditioning in the school seemed to dissuade them. All of us had been inoculated against virtually everything bar dengue fever, and would actually be able to travel almost anywhere in the world in the future.

During this period I very quickly realised what a massive learning curve I was on. I hadn't factored in that many countries had sanctions against Sudan, and weren't prepared to trade with them. I had to boil water to wash the dishes (no dishwasher, and I had to obtain bottled water; not for us the luxury of water from the tap). Our clothes had to be taken to what we would term a laundry, but was actually just a huge bucket of soapy water, which someone poked with what seemed to be a stick; but the clothes amazingly smelt very fresh and were certainly clean.

I could find bread huts and the bread was very nice, but if you didn't visit first thing there would be nothing left. We tended to survive off the local bread wraps, initially, and I found very quickly how hard it was to find nutritious food. I was quite anxious as I felt that we would all fall ill if we couldn't get the right foods. I didn't know what Peter would say about this as in England we could purchase literally anything we wanted. We did find that we were all prone to stomach upsets at one time or another, which seemed to be quite normal in Sudan.

I found it was very difficult to communicate with England from Sudan as there were no landlines, only mobiles. During the two months I was waiting for Peter's arrival, I only managed to speak to him four times. I was very conscious how much a mobile call would be, and the connection for Skype was very hit-and-miss. One conversation remains in my mind. It was three weeks before Peter was to arrive, and we were both very down as we had been apart for two months. Peter asked me if we were doing the right thing. I had to be honest and say I didn't know.

I told him that if it didn't work out, we had only rented our home for six months and we could come back, but we both wanted to give this a shot as we had invested so much. I didn't know how Peter would cope without his creature comforts or indeed how I would, long-term. I was very conscious at this point that my family was entering into unknown territory to give me an opportunity, and the pressure on me was phenomenal.

At this point I knew that I had a few classes in, but didn't know whether this was a flash in the pan or it would continue. The day before Peter was to arrive, I went out again with the driver. I wanted to see if I could find any shops which might have some foods we could find in England. We drove to Omdurman, and I found a tiny shop where I found tins of spam, which isn't the best, but I felt I could cook it if the gas cylinder didn't run out halfway through. I also found a small box of Weetabix, and I was amazed to find a jar of Maxwell House coffee. Later, we were to teach a coffee company English and they did have their own brands, but I missed English coffee. If I visited companies I would be offered a hibiscus drink. Unless you have lived in a country like Sudan, you cannot comprehend how elated you would feel finding these items. A luxury for me was a small bar of soap and a bottle of shampoo.

That day we were driving along, and in a traffic jam which was normal in Sudan, when I spotted a young man walking between the cars with a beautiful Persian rug. I asked my driver Ahmed to ask how much it would cost as I felt it would really brighten up the reception at the school. After much haggling I managed to purchase it at the exorbitant price of £3. This wouldn't be possible in the UK. I would have loved to bring some home to England.

Hopefully, Peter would see what I had tried to do to make it easier for his arrival. As time went on he would often say he couldn't believe how homely I had made it for us, even finding mugs to drink the coffee out of.

Chapter 10

Chinese Contracts

As we had the unique selling point of being native English speakers, we very quickly established our first contracts, but working out the pricing for each course was fraught with difficulties as, although I could work out the courses and the pricing, often Mohammed would come in at the last minute and put the prices up. He didn't think long-term and repeat business; he wanted to achieve as much money as he could on each course. I found myself constantly fighting to ensure a fair price for clients.

From the teachers' point of view we had a set number of teaching hours each week, but on occasions, because of Eid or Ramadan, they were teaching considerably less, but still being paid the same amount. It was extremely difficult for a schedule to be worked out. In addition to this we had agreed that the wages would be paid in sterling, but often Mohammed would try to exchange at a lower rate, and then I would have to intervene on the teachers' behalf. It was nothing short of a miracle to me that we kept our teachers. I think the only reason was that I had negotiated a good package at the beginning; they had their accommodation, inoculations, BUPA, and a good hourly rate. The accommodation was quite basic, but they all had their own space. During my time there I did find better accommodation, but for some reason the teachers elected to stay in the original apartment. I think they had adjusted and felt comfortable in their accommodation.

A few months into our stay, I had a visit from a Chinese man who worked for a Chinese oil company working in Sudan, who wanted English Language lessons for his staff, but this would be in the desert at an oil refinery, and the teachers would need to live there Monday to Friday. I had a meeting with the teachers and they were prepared to do this as it would give them a change of surroundings. They would take turns in doing a week each. I remember the first time when I travelled to the oil refinery, I had to get permission to travel as I would be going through different regions and there were checkpoints on the way. Due to the fact that this was an oil refinery, the security would have to be good. My first trip through the desert was a little hair-raising as there was only myself and the driver. I was thinking "What if the car breaks down in the desert?", but when I arrived there I was amazed there was so much greenery, which I hadn't seen for a while, and the surroundings actually looked very pleasant. I thought I wouldn't mind spending a week here. I felt reassured that the teachers would be comfortable, and there was transport provided from Khartoum each week to the refinery. This was a long-term project which I obtained without Mohammed's input.

On arrival at the oil refinery I was amazed by the accommodation, and felt that the teachers would be very comfortable there as they each had their own room, and there were canteens and cleaners on hand, together with several bathrooms (with hot water). There were canteens for both Chinese and Sudanese staff. The teachers wouldn't go hungry. How on earth had they achieved this in the middle of the desert? The Chinese staff employed there used to spend several months, and then they would go home to China to spend time with their families, similar to staff on an oil rig in the UK. They all really missed their families, but told me that they were the fortunate ones as it meant that they could provide very well for their families. The downside from their point of view was that they didn't know where they were likely to be based, and it could be in a country which was in the midst of a civil war as Sudan had been. Whilst we were there, several were sent to Pakistan, which they were a little anxious about, being another country with strife.

Christopher volunteered to take the first week. I think he was enthusiastic as he loved Chinese food, and there was a Chinese cook there so he could eat with them. Christopher told me that this was one of the best experiences he had in Khartoum. He really enjoyed teaching the Chinese and indeed still does today.

We did also manage to secure many Chinese students that we could teach on a one-to-one basis as they were working in several countries, and as in many English was spoken, they needed to improve their standards. Many of them actually sat the IELTS examinations which is the International Language Testing System, and were very proud when they achieved this examination.

From our point of view we were able to keep the teachers occupied, which was no mean feat. For the first time we were able to work out a schedule, but this was to be short-lived as we had Ramadan and Eid coming soon. I was working so hard, just travelling in the car looking for possible clients. I knew that the only way I could keep us solvent was to not get complacent, but just constantly look for new avenues.

Looking back in hindsight I think many people would have given up before now, but I was determined to try and make a success of it. However, I would say to anyone embarking on this type of venture to find out as much as you can about the region and culture beforehand. I didn't have the time to do this, and if I had I wonder if this story would have been told. I don't regret going as I have many fond memories, but I wish I had been given more time to gain inside knowledge.

What I found extremely hard was that the only rest day was

Friday which was their Sabbath, and often, if we had a student that needed tuition we actually lost that day. When we did have time to relax I used to enjoy walking by the Nile, and every Friday we used to see a man and his camel. He used to bathe in the Nile with his camel, and often he would gesture to us. Peter said he wondered if he was asking to exchange the camel for me. We laughed a lot about this. I wasn't very keen as the man was very old and had no teeth. Some of the young Sudanese man used to come to the river to bathe (sometimes nude, which I found very embarrassing), but we used to walk every Friday we could. Can't think why.

Chapter 11

Peter's Experiences

Peter arrived three months after me, and I met him at the airport. We have touched on his experiences and his involvement in the project, and many people would think: Why did he go? He had a great job, a promising and highly respected career trajectory, and in a lot of ways had finally come to a point where he was beginning to make it on his own, very much his own boss.

There are questions to be asked here, and to be honest I ask them too. I conclude that he came over to support me, as I had always followed him wherever his career led, and he felt this was an opportunity for me to shine. He was promised a degree of incentive to come, and unfortunately that promise didn't transpire. First, there was an offer made to him on our initial visit to become a principal at a business college, which would have meant that he could live and work with us, doing a job that he had always been interested to try. Unfortunately, when he attended the interview it became apparent that the college was just two classrooms, and there was already a director in charge, who was quite hostile towards Peter as he felt that he was about to be ousted from his position. Peter was very highly qualified, and this would continue to be a problem throughout his time in Sudan, as he attended numerous interviews which he was more than qualified for, but no position ever transpired. We never got to the bottom as to why this was a problem, as his skill set could have been extremely useful. For the first time, Peter was at a disadvantage, and I felt extremely guilty as he had come to Sudan to give *me* an opportunity. Over the two years that we were there, I tried on numerous occasions to persuade him to go back to the UK with the understanding that I would fulfil our contract there and then join him.

Realising very quickly that this was the case, Peter dealt with feelings of disillusionment and depression by throwing himself into the affairs of the school, designing courses, teaching Business English to valued clients, and drafting proposals to bring the business in. As we mentioned in the previous chapter, our managing director, who was supposed to be handling the business side, was, to a certain extent, clueless, and Peter would often have to challenge him on ideas that, to be frank, made perfect business sense.

One of Peter's clients was part of the security services, and the only time he could attend lessons was on a Friday, so often we had to forego the day of rest. I remember the first time he came to the school to begin his lessons, a large car drew up with security guards fully armed. It was quite a scary experience. I remember Christopher wanted to walk to the shop, and he was told he couldn't leave the building until the end of the lesson. Peter was asked one time to go to the students' apartment, and the car pulled up with the armed guards and Peter dutifully got in, but he really enjoyed teaching this student as he was very well educated.

Peter attempted to settle into Khartoum life, figuring out the best shops to go to for food, finding the right restaurants, which were very thin on the ground. He did take the Sudanese driving test. This was an interesting experience—four people had to jump in and out of a lead car, and drive in a straight line when prompted to do so by a burly policeman. There was a theory test, too, of about five questions, but essentially just a straight line got you the stamp. I don't think the DVLA would approve of this test, but it seemed to do the job. I think such a test accounted for why people were really good at driving in straight lines, but not good at cornering. Peter became used to this style of driving, but not having a map irritated him somewhat. If you wanted to travel other than the main streets, you wouldn't find any indication of where you were. Often your directions were given as "Look for the donkey carts or falafel place" (falafel are chickpea patties covered in breadcrumbs and fried).

He also became accustomed to the holes in the road, which miraculously appeared after a rainstorm. When you fill in a hole with mud it is assumed that the mud might wash away, but this hasn't reached Khartoum yet. Potholes would just appear as if by magic, and then you would spend time physically pushing your car out of the mud. The only decent road, incidentally, was constructed by Osama Bin Laden's construction firm, but he was forced to leave in the late nineties and nothing seems to have been developed since.

This desire to drive arose, funnily enough, when Peter decided to go for a walk. This was a tricky thing to do at the best of times. Most roads didn't have the luxury of pavements, and you often had to negotiate. In his words, donkey carts just seemed to appear from nowhere. He thought he would take a walk along Nile Street, which is the main street in Khartoum (think of Oxford Street, London, if you will). The only difference, however, is that Nile Street has the presidential palace right in the middle of it, which effectively divides the street in two. Civilians are not allowed to walk through the palace grounds.

Peter came to two guards, and it should be mentioned that guards of the palace sport full military gear, and carry rifles. Upon seeing them, Peter got ready to turn around, but one of the guards said, "Khawaja, wait." Electing not to argue with a guard with a gun, and conscious that he was the only white person around for miles, Peter stood there. The guard proceeded to flag down a pickup truck and say, "You will take the khawaja wherever he wants to go."

The guard gave Peter a smile and waved him off. Peter accepted the lift and, when he reached Jamhoria Street, thanked the driver, and hailed a taxi back. I was becoming quite anxious as he had been away a while, and the story he had to tell didn't fill me with confidence.

As you can see, Peter's story is a classic case of adapting to the ultimate in culture shock, and both I and Chris were amazed at how well he adapted. We used to travel to the nearest shawarma place (a shawarma is a Middle Eastern wrap filled with vegetables, spiced meat and often sour cream). He found a nice pizza restaurant and even ate falafel, which was something he had openly admitted he had no desire to try, but when faced with limited choice you adapt very quickly.

He was becoming very close to us, too, as he had always worked in a very high-powered environment and it left very little time for family; but now he finally had a chance to spend some time and bond with Christopher, which was something that had been very sadly lacking in the past. It was time that we wouldn't have spent in England, and it was made more poignant by the way the story ended.

I think this is probably the point where we should mention how the story ended, because it has relevance to both how the last few months of the story panned out, and how we were influenced as a result of our experience. This trip to Khartoum would turn out to be Peter's last adventure. He developed renal failure whilst there, and passed away in the local teaching hospital.

We will go into more detail toward the end of the book. However, it needs to be said that all the anecdotes so far happened when we didn't know this event was to come, and we weren't prepared for the grief or the upheaval it would cause.

Because of this, the second half of my book is from the perspective of the reader now having this insight, which in many ways enables someone reading this to see the story from my viewpoint, and might provide an extra dimension to my account.

Chapter 12

My Beautiful Flower

When I had been living in Khartoum for a few months, my secretary pointed out to me all the elaborate henna designs which the Sudanese women had on their hands. I had seen henna in England, but nothing like this as some of the designs were beautiful. It was explained to me that often women had this done before their wedding. It was suggested that I might like to have one on my hand as I was now living in Khartoum. My secretary made a telephone call, and Ahmed took me to what I thought was a little hut, but inside there was a Sudanese woman putting a henna picture on a woman's arm. I was fascinated to watch her. It was a beautiful ornate flower. When it was my turn, she pointed to some pictures and asked what I would like. I said I would like a flower similar to the one she had just completed. The actual process was quite long as this was an artist at work, but the finished result was something to behold. I was told it would take a little while to dry so I set off to the market as I needed to source some material so that I could have some skirts made. I was losing quite a lot of weight which was a combination of a limited diet and the heat.

I arrived at the market, and quite quickly found some material that would be suitable, but then was amazed to find that the seamstresses were all men. There were several sewing machines in a line, and they were all busily working. I was told by gestures that one of the men would need to measure me, which I was a little worried about. I was hoping they wouldn't try to take liberties because I didn't have the language skills to reprimand them; just one of the hurdles I had to jump over as a western woman. I did have a few instances where I had to push his hands away, but I coped. I think they were shocked to see a white woman there as we were pretty thin on the ground.

After this I wandered through the market looking to see what was for sale; and if there were any homely things which would make the apartment more like our home in England, then I would get them. I remember Peter saying he couldn't believe how much like home I had made the apartment. It should be noted at this point that we were all homesick as everything we take for granted in England just wasn't there. Since coming back to England I never cease to feel grateful for what we have. I had even found some mugs and, with great difficulty, knives and forks, as in Sudan they eat with their fingers and often off the same plate.

What I didn't know was that, during this time, the school had been ringing my telephone trying to get me to answer. Apparently, you have to wash excess henna off because it can be toxic. Eventually I answered the telephone to Yasir, our manager, who was shouting down the telephone in English, "Wash the excess henna off. Are you feeling okay?" I had a bottle of water with me and some tissues, so I just poured lots of water and rubbed it on. Yasir said it would be a good idea now to come back to the school, still not having actually *told* me that it could be toxic.

I arrived back at the school, and Yasir rushed to me and told me to soak the henna in water, which I did. When it was explained to me what could have happened, I was shocked. Needless to say, I didn't repeat the experience, but I was extremely happy with the design and pleased that I had done it once.

Chapter 13

Archie

A few months after moving to Khartoum I was sat in my Office working out a proposal for a new client and I felt something on my foot. I looked down and was surprised to find a mouse (although it was rather large and could have been a rat). The mouse scurried across the floor and I was so surprised I didn't even scream which probably would have been the normal reaction. I have to say that I had only seen one mouse in my lifetime so it was yet another experience to chalk up to Sudan and this roller-coaster ride I was on.

I went downstairs to have a word with Yasir, my manager, as I wasn't sure what they did to solve this problem. I tried to explain to him about mousetraps and poison in England, and even about us tempting them with cheese, but I hadn't seen any cheese although there were many goats so that cheese could have been a possibility. He told me that the only solution was to get a cat. I wasn't very keen on this as the family had always had dogs even though Peter as a child living above a butchers shop had always had them.

The following morning there was a knock on my Office door and it was our driver holding a black and white cat, but this wasn't a domestic cat as in England it was a feral or wild cat. I had no experience of cats and wondered if I could pet it, but Archie left me in no doubt that I couldn't as when I tried to touch him he spat at me. However, I felt if he solved the problem I could deal with that. My next problem was what on earth do we feed him on as I certainly hadn't seen any shops with cat food in. Our driver told me that Archie was a feral cat and would find his own food, which didn't seem very satisfactory to me. However, in time I found a shop in Omdurman that sold cat food. I think Archie was actually fed better than we were.

As time went on Archie became a little more domesticated. He would allow my son Christopher to pet him and even on occasion would sit on his feet or even on his lap. However, Archie was extremely independent and would often disappear for days on end, but he seemed to realise that the School was now his home and he would reappear as if by magic.

One day I was travelling back from a meeting and I heard the most horrendous screeching I was a little wary not knowing what it was, but then I came upon Archie and another Feral Cat fighting Archie was coming off the worst. We managed to chase away the other cat, but Archie was very badly mauled and I could see the bones in his back. I knew that Christopher would be very upset if Archie died as he had become very attached to him, but I didn't think we would be able to find a vet in Khartoum so was at a loss as to what could be done for now and all we could do was wash his back and bandage it and hope he would recover.

The following day I spoke with one of my students and they told me of what they termed a miracle ointment. This was a Chinese ointment which they used for many ailments and he thought it might work for Archie. I felt that it was worth a go as we had nothing to lose.

Christopher asked if he could tend to Archie and he religiously applied the ointment and changed the bandage every day and gradually Archie recovered, and was back to his independent ways sometimes disappearing for seven days at a time, but he always reappeared.

The overriding memory I have of Archie is when we were leaving Khartoum and he was stood on the wall looking at us. I really wished at that point we could take him home with us, but it would have been impossible as it is hard enough with a domestic cat and I don't know how difficult it would be with a feral cat, and immigration controls.

Chapter 14

Homestay in the UK

It had long been an ambition to send students over to England, and as this was what I had been doing in the UK, it seemed logical that I should take a group there. I was told that this was an extreme honour as they wouldn't just allow anyone to take their students to a foreign country. This pilot group was to be boys only, but if it was successful then a repeat would include girls.

But before we could embark on this trip we had to obtain visas, which was no mean feat. I spent days at the British Embassy answering questions. They wanted to know what was the purpose of the visit, and would they be coming back? I think they were concerned as my group was made up of students from very important families. Eventually we were allowed to go, as the boys were all teenagers and obviously coming back. Mohammed told me that one of the adult students that had recently been studying English with us was to accompany me to assist with the supervision of the students. However, a matter of days before we were to go we found that his visa application had been refused. I was never told why. I was asked if I would consider taking the boys on the trip alone with one of the older boys acting as my assistant. In hindsight, this was probably quite a silly thing to agree to, but I didn't want to disappoint the boys, as some had never visited England.

When we set off from the airport I was a little apprehensive, wondering what a responsibility I had taken on. When we arrived in England I was surprised to find a Sudanese man beckoning us to join another desk at immigration, as the queue for non-European Union nationals was very long; but we walked over and were ushered through customs very quickly with the Sudanese man accompanying us. When I had an opportunity to speak to him, it was explained that he worked at the Sudanese Embassy in London, and he had been dispatched to assist us through customs. He then told me that we had been invited to spend a day at the Sudanese Embassy in London. What I hadn't been told at this juncture was that staff were going to act as security for us.

All the boys were staying with English families whom I had worked with in England, and all of them were very familiar with Sudanese students as they had hosted adults for me before. I still had an assistant in the UK and she was going to help with the stay. However, I just had time to recover from my jet lag when there was a telephone call. One of the families told me that there was a car at the end of the road with two men inside. These would later turn out to be Sudanese, and acting as bodyguards for the student who was staying with them. I hadn't been told this, but you can imagine the problem I had explaining this to the family once I had been told what was going on. The family actually took it very calmly, and they said, "We are extremely safe, aren't we," but it could have been a very different story.

We were to take the boys on different excursions, and one was to London which they were fascinated with. I had to keep a very close eye on them as they kept stopping to look in the various shops. One of the things I remember with some amusement was going into Marks and Spencer's and the boys staring open-mouthed at the lingerie counter; and then one of them took his camera out and started snapping bras. The assistant was looking at me shocked so I explained that in their own country they wouldn't see a department like this. I think at this point I realised how lucky we were in the UK. Even today I thank my lucky stars for hot water, a dishwasher, and all the things we take for granted.

When we were waiting to catch the train to go back, I noticed the boys were looking and pointing at a very pretty girl with a miniskirt on, as in their own country the girls would wear skirts down to the ground, and the tops would be long-sleeved with high necks, and it would be finished with the scarf on their head. For them it was something they had never seen before. It was mentioned to me on several occasions that they felt that there was much more freedom in the UK, which of course there is. I think it must be hard for Sudanese students to come to the UK to study, and then go back to their own country were maybe there is an arranged marriage in the offing.

Very quickly the day dawned when we were to visit the Sudanese Embassy. I had visited before, of course, when I obtained my visa to visit Sudan, but only the immigration department. Today I was to meet the ambassador and his staff and have a tour of the embassy. What an experience; I had never met an ambassador before. I was quite excited. We were to spend the day there and have a buffet lunch which was a combination of Sudanese and English food. The boys really enjoyed the tour of the embassy, and were looking forward to telling their friends when they arrived back in Sudan. All too soon the day was over, and it was time to travel back to the families.

The holiday very soon came to an end, and the boys were full of the things they had done, but looking forward to going home and telling their friends and family about it. I had a few hurdles to jump over yet, as when the boys boarded the coach to travel to the airport, I noticed they had many gifts, one of which was a Hoover, would you believe? I asked the coach driver to wait as I didn't think we would be allowed to take everything on board with the baggage allowance. We arrived at the desk, and I was amazed that everything was allowed through. It was the local Sudanese Airways, so maybe that accounted for it. We proceeded through to departures, and I counted the boys and realised that one was missing. Where was he? One of the other boys said, "He went that way with the Sudanese man who met us at the airport." I asked the boys to wait together whilst I found him. It didn't take long: he was walking to the departure gate. I ran up to them and asked what they were doing. The man said that they had upgraded the seat for the boy. I said, "These boys are in my charge. You can't do that. He will stay with us as I am responsible for him until we arrive back." I took him back to the other boys, not knowing what repercussions this would cause, but quite prepared to accept them.

On the plane flying back, I had time to reflect, and realised what a foolhardy thing it had been to take a group of boys to England alone. I could have lost them, and then what would have happened? Thankfully, they were all present and accounted for, but I would think twice before repeating this.

The plane we travelled back on was a local Sudanese company and very different from our planes. I managed to make sure that all the students were belted up, but I couldn't fasten mine, which was a little scary.

Chapter 15

The Bike and Teddy Bear Incident

When we arrived in Sudan we had had to register at the British Embassy, and then if there was any security risk we would be informed by email. I have to say, during most of my time in Khartoum, I often felt safer than I would have done in the UK, the reason being that the punishments were so severe that people hesitated to do anything against the law. In the main street there were pictures of people in the Secret Service, which I found very surprising as this wouldn't happen in the UK.

However, two incidents remain in my memory. The first was when a refugee stole a bicycle from the school, and our caretaker caught him and called the police. The policeman wanted to put him in prison, and he said the punishment for stealing was to lose a hand. I said, "I am not going to press charges. I will give him jobs to do in the school." To my amazement he agreed, but Peter said afterwards I had taken quite a risk as I could have been arrested too. The refugee was only a teenager and he must have been desperate to do this.

The second time was infinitely more scary as I received an email from the embassy to tell me that an English teacher working at a local Sudanese school had been arrested as she had named a teddy bear Mohammed, which was extremely disrespectful in Sudan. Apparently there were due to be demonstrations in Jamhoria Street, and we were advised to stay indoors. I walked up to the roof of the school, and I could see the demonstration. All I could hear was shouting, and see people waving their hands about, but I was careful not to be seen. The poor woman was thankfully in prison only for a few days, and then released and deported. However, it later transpired that it wasn't her that had named the teddy bear, but the students. One of the staff members must have had some sort of a grudge against her and the school as she reported her.

I received a telephone call from a journalist asking for a comment. I had already advised the teachers not to discuss the matter. I asked him, "How can I comment when I live here? There could be repercussions against myself and the school." I later found out that Mohammed in his infinite wisdom had given the journalist my number. Needless to say, we had quite a discussion about this.

That week I went to a usual get-together at the embassy, and they were talking about this, and were very upset that it had happened, but it brought home to me and our teachers how very precarious our situation was, and how we had to be very careful what we did.

Chapter 16

Eid Trip to Port Sudan

We had all been working extremely hard, and we didn't have any students coming in over Eid, which was also our Christmas, so we decided to have a family trip to Port Sudan. Initially, we had thought that we would fly, but unfortunately there were no planes during the Eid period so Mohammed suggested that we hire a Landcruiser and driver. We thought that this would be a chance to see more of Sudan. Mohammed had arranged for us to stay with a relative of his when we arrived at Port Sudan, so I thought that it would be a nice experience. We had to obtain all the relevant permissions to travel to Port Sudan, which would normally take months, but due to the assistance of our friends these were rushed through.

The plan was that we would drive down to Kassala, see this, and then head down to Port Sudan. It should have been a trip to remember, and in hindsight it was, but not for the reasons we anticipated. The itinerary was fantastic as we were going to see Sugarloaf Mountain on the way, so named because it was shaped like colonial sugarloaves. Port Sudan was luring us with the promise of cheap lobster. As our diet in Sudan was extremely limited, this would be some treat.

We started our adventure exploring the desert and what were areas of lush greenery; but suddenly we came to a bump in the road, and the car jolted in the air and landed with a thud. This is the best argument in the world for wearing seat belts. Sudanese often don't wear them as they feel what will be will be. This often meant that car accidents were normally quite grisly and, unfortunately, a few hours later we were about to find out how grisly. Thankfully we were all wearing seat belts, but the driver declined, and I often wonder, if he had done, perhaps he wouldn't have been as badly injured.

As we approached the road that would take us to Kassala, we came onto a stretch with a market. There we were made aware that a pickup truck had stopped in the road in such a way that we had to stop for them (in other words, making a deliberate roadblock). "Bandits," the driver said, and he swerved to avoid them; but a truck was coming the other way and hit us head on.

It should be mentioned at this point that Peter and I were in the back and Christopher was in the front, and I am sure that some readers will sympathise with that split second when you worry that you may have lost a child. On that basis, the relieved surprise when I heard Chris say, "Right, there is oil leaking. Get your f...ing belts off now!" went part of the way to dealing with the shock. I didn't feel this was an appropriate time for reprimanding him about his language. Luckily, a local shepherd ran to the car and helped me out of it. The kindness this shepherd showed me I will never forget. He insisted on giving me a drink of water, and then he noticed I had lost one of my shoes, and went back to the car to get it for me with no thought for his own safety. The story from there is a bit of a blur. Chris told me that the driver went through the windscreen, and that was when he smelt the oil leaking from the engine. It should be said that many of the villagers tried to help us, and guided us to the market so that we could see what was unfolding.

The truth was that at this stage both myself and Peter were experiencing a feeling of powerlessness. Peter had fainted, and I was so worried about the driver. I didn't even know whether he was still alive. Chris, on the other hand, not to say he wasn't worried, seemed to take charge. He had been helped on to the top of a truck, trying to find a signal on his mobile to get us help. I was so proud of him at this point.

Whilst we waited, and Chris attempted to negotiate everything in a language he didn't speak very well, Peter and I were being thoroughly checked over by an Ethiopian doctor, who was basically jumping over the border to obtain a better salary. By the way, if you are thinking the sort of security you would have at Dover, think again. This particular border is just four trees, and although he never told me at the time, Chris actually backed over it by mistake. The doctor shouted, "Walk forward now. You have a minute before the Ethiopian border force may fire at you."

The ambulance came, and we were rushed to Kassala Hospital. The doctors were very dedicated there, but it should be mentioned that the facility was extremely basic as it was a field hospital. And to those people who actually think the commercials on television asking for support are exaggerating, you couldn't be further from the truth. Even basic painkillers were hard to come by. What you have to remember at this point is that Sudan had been in the grip of a civil war for twenty-five years.

Peter was examined, but I wouldn't be treated until I knew everyone was okay. The trouble was that my instinct to look after everyone before myself wasn't necessarily the right thing here. Christopher argued with me in the hospital. "Look, you need help; stop resisting and get yourself to a doctor," he said, but I wasn't prepared to take his advice. As it turned out, his assessment was fair as I collapsed on the floor and took him with me. Ironically, that caused most of his bruising, not the truck.

As you have probably gathered, this is a time when I remember feeling a sense of pride in my son's conduct, but the final flourish was the most striking still. Once everyone had been treated, he ran out of the hospital door, and pulled out his camera. The doctor came out and said, "Sir, we have to check you over" to which he replied, "Look, you can wait a couple of minutes. I came here for a photo of Sugarloaf Mountain, and I am getting one." In some ways it felt like a just reward for the way he had behaved that day, like he had earned that photo; and actually we still look at it as a reminder of how lucky we were.

In the interim, Peter had regained consciousness in the hospital, and had to process this rather smiley doctor saying to him, "Okay, your wife passed out, but she fine now. One shot of adrenaline and she chipper." In the meantime, Christopher came to me and told me that men had arrived from the local security services to take us back to Khartoum as Mohammed, together with a large group of our students and friends, had arranged this. They had planned to take just us back, but I was adamant that the driver should come too if it was safe for him to do so, as I wasn't sure he would survive in Kassala Hospital. I wanted to try and get him into one of Khartoum's better clinics, In the end, I won this dispute.

Chapter 17

The Journey Back to Khartoum and the Aftermath

An ambulance arrived at Kassala Hospital as we were to travel throughout the night. Our driver was on a stretcher, and I was just so relieved to see that he was still alive, albeit swathed in bandages. My worry about leaving him there was that it was miles from Khartoum, and his family probably wouldn't be able to visit him. His only concern was that we were safe, but his screams still haunt me. He was in agonising pain, having broken countless bones in several places. The journey took twelve hours, and he needed painkillers constantly because the roads were very bad, and every bump jolted him. I was so scared that he wouldn't last the journey as I had insisted we bring him. Had I made the right decision?

When we eventually arrived back in Khartoum, he was taken to the Chinese Hospital as this was open, and they were carrying out operations in the Eid period. This, I think, is what saved his life as they were able to operate very quickly, and in time he made a full recovery.

The following day, it was decided that we should attend a clinic to be checked over. During the night several massive bruises had appeared on my body. Some of them were seat belt injuries, but better that and being alive. We flagged down a taxi only for him to drive very fast and erratically, and he almost caused an accident. I didn't realise that I was still in shock, and started screaming, "Let me out." We got out of the taxi and quickly flagged down another one, who thankfully drove very safely once he was told what had happened.

We arrived at the hospital, and I was ushered into the doctor who seemed shocked to see a western woman. I later found out that male doctors don't normally treat women. He asked me if my massive bruise was a "tattoo" and if all western women had them. Slapping him probably didn't help the situation, but it made me feel better.

As for Peter, he had broken a rib and he had minor whiplash, but thankfully Christopher had adopted the recovery position at the time of the crash. In the aftermath Christopher was suffering from emotional scars as he couldn't forget the moment the driver went through the windscreen. When the driver had recovered sufficiently, we arranged for Peter and Christopher to visit him so that Christopher could be reassured that he was okay. Even then, all he was thankful for was that *we* were okay.

The other incident that happened at this time was that our manager Yasir, who accompanied us, had a recurring malaria attack. This was the first time I had seen this, but it wasn't to be the last. Yasir was in the grip of a fever with a very high temperature, and didn't seem to know where he was. The nurse gave him an injection and told him to go home and rest. My father had been based in Malaysia during his National Service, and I remember my Mum telling me that not long after she had met him, he had an attack on the bus and she had to take him home. I now understood what she'd meant about the fever and the glassy eyes staring straight ahead.

What an eventful few days—and we never actually saw Port Sudan.

Chapter 18

Our Holiday

We had been in Sudan for over a year and were feeling a little tired and jaded, and desperately needed a holiday. We had worked six days, sometimes seven, every week, and I had been working from 4 a.m. every morning until sometimes 10 p.m. (although this wasn't strictly true, as often the students would come up to our apartment wanting to talk, and we never had the heart to say we were tired. I loved my job and wasn't complaining, but Peter felt that if I carried on this way I would very quickly burn out. What I didn't really take on board was that each day I was working double what I would have done in the UK. Although I had my homestay in the UK. I didn't work consistently; I would have rest times, whereas this was busy all the time, because even when the students weren't there, I had to try and source other business just to keep us afloat.

We decided that we would like to spend a week in Jordan on a tailor-made holiday, as we felt we deserved it. One of our dreams had always been to see some of the wonders of the world, and Petra seemed a very good place to start. However, it was going to prove extremely problematical to even get a visa, the problem being that my work visa was due to be renewed, and what I thought would be a simple matter was extremely complicated as the immigration department spent weeks deliberating as to whether to extend it. I think if I had been open to bribery this could probably have been sorted; but, being married to a barrister, this was never on the cards. However, we had a brainwave. What if we applied for a temporary holiday visa, and figured out the renewal details on our return... but, unfortunately, the brainwave occurred after we had missed our plane.

We were determined to have a holiday so we went to the Royal Jordanian Offices in Khartoum, and asked if we could obtain seats on their next plane, which was the following day. Thankfully we could, but they only had business class. This would be the first time either of us had travelled this way, and we were quite excited to know what the difference was. The journey was excellent, with nothing being too much trouble for the staff.

We flew to Amman where we would meet Ibrahim who was to be our driver for the whole of our stay. As we had very limited time, only having six days, we wanted to experience as much as we possibly could. Our first port of call was Petra, and we would stay two nights there so that we could enjoy both a day trip to the Siq and then an evening seeing it by candlelight, which was quite magical. In the evening we walked the entire Siq to the Treasury which is lit by over 1,000 candles, and then we all sat cross-legged by the Treasury and listened to the traditional music. At the end of the day we just fell into bed as we were exhausted.

The following day Ibrahim, our driver, took us to Wadi Rum where we met with a Bedouin guide who drove us in a Land Rover through the rocky landscape. He explained that today the King of Jordan has made a settlement for the Bedouins in Wadi Rum, but they still like to travel and use this as their base. We looked at the places where they lived, and visited a cultural market which was extremely interesting. In addition to the tour we took you could also have spent a few days exploring or experiencing some of the fun activities such as ballooning, and we felt that we would come again in the future, but maybe stay a few days at Wadi Rum.

The following day we were to spend a few nights at the Hotel Kempinski, which was situated on the banks of the Dead Sea. One of our most enjoyable experiences was floating in the Dead Sea. We had to coat ourselves in mud, and then walk into the sea and float. Apparently, the water is supposed to have many health benefits. I took a bottle home for my Mum as she suffered from arthritis and psoriasis. She said she did feel better, so hopefully it did some good.

The hotel itself was the height of luxury. Our room had absolutely everything you would need. The shampoos and shower gel smelt lovely, and your hair and skin felt really clean and soft afterwards. After being in Sudan for over a year this was heaven, and I just wanted it to last for ever. It gave Peter and I chance to relax, and I think in some ways we had forgotten how to do this. The hotel itself had nine pools, a fitness centre, and a tennis court. To relax there were four restaurants and a bar. It was billed as a seven-star hotel, and I could see why.

We concluded our stay back in Amman, staying at the Marriott Hotel for our final day. This would be our opportunity to explore this beautiful city. What we wanted to do was to visit some of the religious and cultural buildings, but as it was a Friday many of them were closed. However, at the Amman Citadel, we met a nice young Jordanian policeman, who kindly offered to show us around. While we were there, Peter took a photograph of me with the policeman, and a woman came up to us and said to our guide, "You should marry her—nice English lady—ask her father over there." I and Peter were mortified at first, but afterwards we both saw the funny side.

In the evening we visited a souk (a market) which had many small stalls including pottery and jewellery, and we found a lovely stall selling jewellery, and Peter treated me to a necklace, bracelet, and earrings which were in the shape of a butterfly. The jewellery was quite expensive, but we were able to haggle and obtain a reduced price. It was our wedding anniversary; we had been married thirty years so Peter felt this was a fitting treat. We then had a very special meal in the restaurant. I have such wonderful memories of this holiday.

The following day we were to fly home, but I wanted to treat Peter to something before we left. I asked Ibrahim if there was somewhere I could buy Peter a nice watch. He took me to a jewellers, and I found a very nice watch which I could have engraved when we eventually travelled home to England. Neither of us was looking forward to the trip back to Sudan; this holiday had reminded us what we had given up.

When we arrived back, Peter left feedback on the Tourism Agency Website:

Dear Lamees

We returned from holiday on Sunday morning. and we are now back at work after Eid. We had an excellent holiday. and thank you very much for organising such an interesting itinerary. Thank you particularly for rearranging the itinerary at such short notice after we missed the plane.

Our driver Ibrahim Alsmadi, was excellent, and we would be happy to have him as our driver when we come again. [Notice he said *when*, not *if*.] Petra was very interesting, but, much to our surprise, it was by no means the best part of the holiday. Wadi Rum and the Kempinski Hotel were excellent. We saw Petra by day and night on the same day. Both trips were well worthwhile, but we would just suggest that you warn people walking trips into the Siq (and especially back again) can be very tiring.

We are thinking ahead to the Ramadan period next year (this seems a quiet period for the hotels), and we are considering a trip based on the Kempinski Ishtar (which really is very good indeed). We saw most of the sights on this holiday, but we would like another visit to Wadi Rum, perhaps for longer, and including sight of the sunset. We would also need transport to and from the hotel and to Wadi Rum. However, we are also open to suggestions of places we haven't seen. Could you give us some ideas for an itinerary and prices based on this information—staying at least a week, and then perhaps a price for each extra night.

In many ways this is a fitting way to document what turned out to be a last trip together, but it does get across how suddenly the situation changed. As you can see, even at this stage he was thinking about a holiday for the next year.

Chapter 19

The Bright Future of Winner

We now take ourselves to the beginning of November 2007, and the future for 'Winner' looked extremely bright. I had been negotiating with logistics companies, and we had designed a course specifically for this industry. If they wanted to extend their businesses, they needed to improve their English. At this point we had run a pilot course which had been very successful, and we were looking to branch out to other areas of Khartoum with our teachers working at their premises. I was looking to negotiate a very lucrative contract designing specialist English courses for the haulage industry. I was very excited about this breakthrough as I felt that if it worked for the haulage industry, it could work for other industries. This was a culmination of all the hard work over the two years we had been there.

Unfortunately, it was also at this time that I began to notice changes in Peter's health. It should be mentioned that we were all prone to stomach upsets in Khartoum due to water quality and the lower levels of sanitation, but in mid-November Peter found himself having to leave classes so that he could be sick. He started to look paler, and was losing weight and feeling exhausted. I was becoming extremely worried about him, and I wanted him to seek medical help, but he said he was fine. He didn't trust much of the food so would only eat at certain places. On many occasions I used to bring food up in an attempt to get him to eat, but as time progressed he kept refusing it. I managed to get him to visit the doctor eventually, and he prescribed the normal medication for an upset stomach. For a while Peter was better, but I worried about his health and wanted him to go back to England to further his consultancy career, and have his health checked. It took me some time as he refused to leave us in Khartoum, but I managed to persuade him, and told him that I would only stay in Khartoum for the time it took me to recruit another director, and then I would join him. He had promised me that as soon as he arrived back in England he would seek treatment, and hopefully be okay.

However, Peter wanted to have Christmas with the family before he flew back, which seemed a reasonable request. We actually had pizza for Christmas dinner as there was no way we would find turkey there, and stayed up late watching reruns of *House MD*, Peter's favourite programme when we were in Khartoum. It was very difficult to source TV programmes as these were normally satellite, illegal, imports. Unfortunately, Peter became ill again, but wouldn't go to hospital so I sat up with him all night. It was one of those life-changing evenings, and we spent most of the night talking about our son, and what he would do in the future. We also talked about what *we* would do in the future, Peter felt that Christopher had a gift for teaching, and this is what he should pursue. Peter had always had a dream to retire to Lanzarote, and we discussed that he would cut down his hours with a view to retiring in a few years and then following the dream. It was a major turning point for Peter as he had always worked long and hard, and even at this point we didn't know how belated it would prove.

The next day, Peter became very sick indeed. We phoned Yasir, our manager, and he came immediately. We carried Peter on a stretcher to the van, bound for the teaching hospital in Khartoum. He had several tests that day, and although there was a need for more to be carried out, the initial results never came to us. This was the first time I realised how serious the situation had become. I was beside myself with worry.

When I visited Peter with Christopher the day after, he told me he may have to go on dialysis for a time as his kidneys had not been functioning properly. He looked unwell, but told us he felt a little better. I told him we would work it out, whatever treatment he needed. I will never know the extent to which he was trying to reassure us. I left that visit thinking 'Thank God we have repatriation with BUPA' as I felt I needed to get him home, and at this point I stated that I wasn't staying in Khartoum; I was going home with him as he was the most important thing to me. I wasn't allowed to stay in the ward with him as local custom forbade it. In hindsight, now, I wish I had just organised the plane there and then, but I think it was probably too late. People say to me when it is your time, there is nothing you can do, but I will always beat myself up wondering if I could have done more. Peter was my rock. How would I cope without him if I lost him?

Chapter 20

The End of the Family as we Knew it

Peter had been in hospital one day, and I had left my telephone number with them and asked them to contact me if there was any change. I went back to the school and carried on with my work as I felt it was better to be busy. I went to bed a little after 10 p.m., as was usual, but around 11 p.m. I woke suddenly, which was rather unusual for me as I am normally a heavy sleeper, and had a strange urge to sort through our papers. I didn't know why, but this carried on for a few hours. I even tried to wake Christopher up to assist, but he was fast asleep. By 3 a.m., though, I had a telephone call, in broken English, and I just knew, but don't know to this day how, that it was about Peter. I said, "It's my husband, isn't it? What's happened?" The only reply I kept getting was "hello". I screamed down the telephone, "Stop saying hello and tell me what has happened." The person on the other end of the telephone said, "I'm sorry" and then proceeded to tell me that Peter had just died. I just threw the telephone, and ran to Christopher's room, thumping on the door as hard as I could until he woke up. I didn't think there was a right way of telling him this news, and I was in a state of shock myself. I tried to stay calm and just said, "Chris, I have some very sad news. Unfortunately, your Dad has passed away." Christopher came rushing out screaming, saying it must be a mistake. I tried to calm him and gather my thoughts together.

I made a telephone call to our driver and Yasir, our manager, who travelled to the school and took us to the hospital. When we arrived we were taken to the ward where a Filipino nurse was waiting for us. He told us that he didn't have our telephone number even though we had left it with them, and apologised for the way his Sudanese co-staff were organised. I snapped at him, which I regret now as it wasn't his fault; he tried really hard to help. I asked him what would have happened if Peter had no relatives in Khartoum. Apparently, he would just have been sent to the embassy, and they would have handled the repatriation. As a final, lasting memory, the nurse went on to describe Peter as a gentleman who was very grateful for his help, and thanked him. In the end, he said, it had been peaceful; he had just drifted off to sleep. He asked if I would like to see him, and I said yes. Peter looked as if he was just sleeping, and that was of some comfort.

At this point Yasir came in and handed me the telephone. Mohammed was on the line. He callously told me that he didn't think we had enough health insurance to get Peter home. We wouldn't have had, but often I didn't take a wage in order to pay BUPA as I knew how important it was. Wrong time, wrong place, and wrong sentiment. It should be stated at this point that Mohammed did not convey his condolences, and indeed he never would.

There was nothing more we could do at that time. The nurse told us that later that day I would need to go to the embassy and register Peter, and obviously start the long and complicated process of getting Peter home, which I was determined to do as I knew Peter would not want to be buried in Sudan.

I and Christopher, still in a state of shock, were driven back to the school. We were exhausted, and knew that we needed to rest, but how could we, given what had happened? We didn't want to be alone, so both lay on the bed talking about Peter and how we would miss him. Peter had not just been a loving husband; he had been my best friend, my rock, and my mentor for over thirty years. How was I going to survive without him? But I knew I had to be strong if I was to get him home so I took a deep breath and put myself on autopilot.

The following morning, Yasir and Sandra, one of our teachers, arrived. Sandra had been through something similar as her father had been a missionary, and had been speaking in Europe when he had passed away, and she proved invaluable as she had a knowledge of the hoops I would have to jump through, although not in a country like Sudan. Sandra told me that when I arrived back in the UK the coroner would probably request an autopsy as Peter had died overseas.

Chapter 21

The Mortuary

The hospital told me that Peter would need to be removed as they needed the bed and asked me what I wanted to do. If the funeral was to be in Khartoum then it would have to be arranged very quickly because of the heat.

Even though I was very shocked and distressed I knew in my own mind that Peter would have wanted to go home to England, but how was I going to achieve this? I just knew that this was what I was going to do. I asked if there was a local mortuary and found there was, but it was very small and they didn't know whether there would be room. I asked them to telephone and thankfully there was and it would give me a little time to make arrangements. The hospital transported Peter to the mortuary.

I told the Filipino nurse at the hospital that I intended to take Peter back to England. He told me it would be very difficult to do if not nigh on impossible, but as you will see in my further chapters I did indeed manage to do this.

Peter needed to be prepared for the travel to England and the mortuary asked me for some clothes. Peter had a favourite short sleeved shirt which I felt he would have wanted. The following day I received a telephone call from the Mortuary asking me to visit to make sure I was happy with everything they had done. At this point I was on automatic pilot as I just knew I had to be strong to get through the coming days.

I arrived at the Mortuary with Christopher and was directed to a room where there were three Sudanese men dressed in the traditional white robes looking on anxiously. I looked at Peter and he seemed to be asleep and looked at peace. I wanted to touch him and tell him to wake up maybe all this was some horrible dream. I felt myself start to shake and then great sobs came from what I later found was myself this was the only time prior to the funeral that I actually broke down. The men looked really upset I think they felt that they had done a bad job, but it was just I was so thankful for what they had been able to achieve. I said thank you and smiled at them and I hope I managed to make them understand how grateful I was to them. We had come to Sudan as a family to hopefully assist them and now in my time of need so many were helping us.

Chapter 22

Then Came the Hard Bit

Before I start talking about how we got Peter home, it should be mentioned that we had made many friends in Sudan. Whilst some people did their utmost to put barriers in front of us to stop us leaving Sudan, others tried to make it as easy as possible. If it weren't for them, to achieve what we eventually did would have been nothing short of miraculous.

The following morning, barely hours after hearing the news of Peter's death, we went to the British Embassy to register his death. We were told immediately that all they could offer was advice. We were given names of funeral directors that worked overseas, and they allowed us to telephone them from their office. However, one piece of information which proved to be very important was that we could have a death certificate in English. Apparently this was a legal requirement, when recording the events of the day before, with a number of official organisations as it allowed Peter's death to be registered in the correct citizenship. I should add at this point that Peter is still not eligible to be registered at Somerset House, London as he died overseas.

We left the embassy, and our next port of call was the morgue. I would just say at this point that there was only one in Khartoum, and we were very lucky to get a place as, because of the climate and culture people are buried very quickly. When I arrived I was met by a man who the funeral directors had cited as their representative. Upon asking about this, though, the man became furious, started shouting, and said quite forcefully that he "wasn't the representative, but a doctor in Sudan." I am sure many people reading this will sympathise with my view that, frankly, I couldn't be interested in debating his credentials. All I was worried about was how I could get Peter home, and to me at this point his credentials didn't matter, but the experience caused yet more grief. Having dealt with this person's wounded pride moment, I then proceeded to tell him that I wanted to take Peter back to England. In response he said, "Well, it would be a bit difficult to do this from our mortuary as all the coffins are made from light wood, and so substandard for air travel." Luckily, I didn't give up, and telephoned the embassy, and they did have a coffin which I would need to pay for, but that was the least of my worries. However, this wasn't the end of the story because we now had to find a vehicle that could carry the coffin as Peter was very tall. Eventually the embassy provided us with one. At this point you are probably thinking, "But the embassy couldn't help". However, an official based there agreed to assist me with transport to the airport together with the paperwork formalities, and I will remain forever grateful for his help.

Elsewhere, however, there was another problem looming as the funeral director I had asked for help telephoned to say that he was having difficulty getting permission for Peter to fly home from any of the flight companies on account of alleged superstition about carrying a deceased person. He said he didn't know whether he could assist, but in my view he had washed his hands of the affair. I had no idea at this point how I would get Peter home, but I was determined to do so.

Enter our local travel agent on Jamhoria Street, to whom we remain indebted. An Egyptian friend of the school, he, surprisingly, knew what to do where the funeral directors did not. Pulling a number of favours in, while I sat in his office for many hours, he arranged the flight to Dubai, the transfer from Dubai to England, and cut through the red tape with regard to Peter travelling through the airports. The final flourish, which ordinarily airlines would not allow (having the body and the relatives on the same flight), we were allowed to do. He admitted later, though, that this was the biggest favour he had ever had to pull. I waited, and then we had a telephone call to say that the flight was arranged for the following day. However, I would have to pay the flights initially, and claim back off BUPA later. The flights were very expensive as not only was I paying for myself and Christopher, but also for Peter. Before I visited the bank he asked me if I had thought as to how I was to transfer my wages to England. Apparently this was extremely difficult, and he offered to arrange the transfer for me if I gave him my bank details in the UK. I trusted him, and didn't have any problem in handing him my wages, which were in excess of £15k. With everything going on, I hadn't thought about how I was going to live in England as our house in Essex was rented out. Of course it was something I should have done, but the most important thing was to get Peter back.

I then had to go back to the school and sort out our belongings, but the first thing I had to do was to telephone my parents and tell them what had happened. My Mum just said, "Get yourself home. You don't need to be there at this time; you need to be home with your family." I explained that we had a flight to Manchester the following day, and Peter would be transported with us. I had arranged for a funeral director to collect Peter from Manchester Airport, and transport him to the funeral directors in Bury, Lancashire, which was where my parents lived, and both Peter and I had grown up there. When I look back on this, I cannot believe that we managed to get Peter home within two days, bearing in mind that we were living in a Third World country. I think Peter would have been very proud of us.

As we had been living in a very hot climate we only had clothes suitable for this weather, and as both of us had lost a lot of weight as the diet was very limited. I can still remember my parents' faces when they collected us from the airport. I was wearing a thin cotton top with a long skirt and sandals, and Christopher was just in a short-sleeved shirt and trousers, hardly the clothing for an English January. Mum later said that we looked like two waifs and strays.

However, before I could actually board the plane I had a few hurdles to overcome. We were due to be at the airport in one hour when I was summoned to my office by Mohammed. All the Board were seated there, and they all gave me their condolences, but not Mohammed. Up to this point he had barely spoken to me, and I said, "I hope you don't mind, but I have a plane to catch to take my husband back to England." Mohammed said, "How many weeks do you need before you return?" I felt I had to be totally honest, so I said, "I don't know when I will return, or even if I will, but if not, I will recruit a manager for you!". As we were in the car to travel to the airport, he said to Christopher, "Don't forget, Christopher— we are your family too. Come back", which I thought in the circumstances was pretty disgraceful as our family had just been ripped apart.

I said I was sorry, but I had to go to the airport otherwise we would miss the plane; and I would be in touch. I will always remember our teachers and Sudanese staff standing waving to us, and then we were off to the airport. When we were seated on the plane, I was sat next to a Red Cross employee, and she talked to me the whole of the journey. In hindsight, I think maybe the airport staff had arranged this as they were worried that I might be upset and cause a scene, but I was just on autopilot, thinking of what I had to do when I arrived back in the UK.

When the plane touched down we met my parents and travelled back to their home, but later that day I was telephoned by the funeral director who had collected Peter, and apparently they had transported him now, but there had been a delay as the customs had to check if Peter's coffin was carrying drugs as we had travelled from Africa. Peter would have been mortified at this, being a qualified barrister and always being careful not to do anything wrong in the eyes of the law.

Chapter 23

Appointment of New Director

After we arrived home I kept expecting to hear from David, the consultant who had asked us to go to Sudan in the first place. I couldn't understand why I hadn't heard anything as he lived in England, and I expected at the very least he would want to come to Peter's funeral, but I heard nothing for some weeks. I asked Mohammed at the time of Peter's death if he knew, and he told me he had telephoned him.

During our time in Khartoum, when he visited he always came to see us, and sometimes we would go out for a meal with him to the Hilton Hotel, which was often used as the hotel that people from the African Congress stayed in when visiting for meetings. I felt that we had become quite good friends, but now I was beginning to wonder if he had been using us to suit his purpose. He acted as a consultant for some important people in Sudan, and was quite highly thought of. Mohammed in a way I could understand, as he was a director of the school as I was, and he probably thought I was letting him down by going home to England, but I couldn't have stayed as there were just too many painful memories.

I decided that the best thing I could do was appoint a new director, and even though there was so much grief in my life, that's what I did. In truth, it actually gave me something to do. I advertised for a new director, and although I interviewed several, there were only a few that would fit the bill as they had to be very adaptable. After compiling a shortlist, the one that most appealed to me was in his fifties, which I didn't see a problem with as I was almost fifty. However, Mohammed felt he was a little too old, I think probably because of what had happened to Peter. I eventually managed to find a director in his thirties from South Africa, and with Mohammed's agreement I recruited him to take over from me. However, in hindsight, what we had done was make the "Winner" part of our family, and it would be very difficult for anyone to take the helm. I think the director found the position very difficult even with my assistance, but it may have been the Mohammed effect. Unfortunately, he only lasted a matter of months, and then we had a succession of directors, not one of them prepared to stay the course.

Initially, when I returned to England, I didn't feel able to talk to Mohammed as I felt he had been extremely insensitive, but I did correspond by email. Eventually I felt able to speak to him again, but I felt very let down As we were leaving Khartoum, he had given Christopher his wages, but it was in Sudanese currency, and of course you can't exchange this in the UK, nor indeed purchase it. Anyone travelling to Sudan is advised to take foreign currency: ideally, US dollars. I think he did this because even at this point he hoped that if I didn't come back, Christopher would. Christopher felt the same as myself, though: that we couldn't go back, only forward, and we both thought that was what Peter would have wanted us to do. In time Christopher managed to obtain his wages in English currency, and indeed a reference, but it took a while for the bad taste to go away as we had worked so hard for them. I am not in contact with Mohammed now, but I don't wish him any ill will.

David the consultant eventually contacted me, and told me that he didn't deal with death very well, and that was why he hadn't telephoned earlier. From my point of view it just wasn't a good enough reason; if something similar had happened to him I would have been on the telephone straightaway. However, I did tell him about Christopher's wages, and maybe he had something to do with Christopher eventually receiving them. I understand that some people don't deal well with these situations, but I am no longer in contact with him either, which is a shame as I felt we had become friends.

The person that remained steadfast in this was Ghani, who actually telephoned and told me he wanted to come to Peter's funeral. At the time he was working as a journalist in London for a Sudanese newspaper, but unfortunately his coach was delayed, and he missed the funeral; but he was there to support us. I still remember my parents' neighbours telling me of a man praying in the street. He telephoned me as he was at Mum's house and didn't know where the funeral was. We were all getting in the funeral cars, so I asked the undertakers to take a slight detour and collect Ghani. Goodness knows what Mum's neighbours thought when the car pulled up and Ghani got in, but I will always appreciate what he did.

Chapter 24

Talking to the Family and Arranging the Funeral

Peter had never been one for keeping in touch with everyone, unlike me. I always remember Mum telling me that Peter had told her that "My family is Janet and Christopher." This being the case, although he had met Tony, his brother, by chance in London before he joined us in Khartoum, he had only mentioned it in passing, and Tony thought he was going on holiday to Khartoum, not to live there. It came as a tremendous shock to both Tony and Steven, his other brother, when they heard the news that Peter had died. I tried to explain what had happened, but I was in a state of shock myself, and probably didn't explain it as well as I could have done. At one point I felt that I was being interrogated by Tony and his wife, but I realise now that they just didn't understand what had happened. I wish it was possible to turn the clock back as I would have dealt with this very differently.

Before I could make the arrangements for his funeral I received a telephone call from the coroner. He had to be satisfied that there were no suspicious circumstances with regard to Peter's death, as his death had been very sudden, in Africa, and there was no paper trail (as there would have been in England) as to what had happened. I did have the death certificate from the British Embassy in Khartoum, in English, which was sufficient in the end. I felt that neither I nor Christopher could bear to have a post mortem as we had been through so much. Once this had been discussed, I was then able to organise Peter's funeral, which I wanted to be a celebration of his life, not a sad occasion.

When Peter was young he had performed a critical assessment of crematoria for a position he had in local government, and concluded that being cremated was the best way forward for him, largely because it was easier for relatives to maintain the plot, although being Catholic by religion he would normally be buried.

I wanted him to be near to where his roots were, so I arranged a ceremony at the local crematorium with an amazing view of Holcombe Hill one of the major landmarks in Greater Manchester. Peter spent his childhood near there, and used to regularly walk up the hill. It felt like a fitting place for Peter to rest. The ceremony was beautiful; everyone walked in to the song "Angels" by Robbie Williams, the priest gave a very appropriate sensitive send-off, and Christopher wrote and delivered a very powerful eulogy which had us all in tears. The brothers were supportive, and asked to read at the service. I feel we all did our best to make sure he went out the right way, as the coffin moved through, and Frank Sinatra's "My Way" became his departure piece. The service was packed with many of his contacts from the magistrates courts and Transport for London. I still visit his memorial every couple of weeks and take flowers. Peter would have said, "Why buy flowers? They are a waste of money." He never bought me flowers when he was alive, but it makes me feel better. I still converse with him about what Christopher is up to, as I feel sure that he is watching over us.

Below is Christopher's eulogy.

Today is a sad day in many respects, but it is also the day to celebrate the life of a very remarkable man. My father, Peter, was a very unique talent, very bright, as the several degrees to his name testified; very successful, very well thought-of, but not in the least bit arrogant. He was a man of distinction, a man of influence, but more important than all these attributes, he was a man of integrity. His ethics played a key role in his decisions, and he always sought a fair resolution to a problem, even if it meant more complications at his end.

As a Chinese student that we taught in Sudan, Sun, once told me, "Mr Peter is a true professional; a gentleman in the most traditional of senses" and he was. He came to Khartoum to support his family, he taught me almost everything he knew, and I will carry what I learnt from him for the rest of my days.

I have so many fond memories of him: when he used to recount the story of me peeing in his face as a baby; when he grimaced as I talked about the priest "handing out crisps" after I had seen Holy Communion for the first time; when he played me "Stairway to Heaven" when I was 14, after despairing at the way my taste in music was going.

In many ways I'm not dissimilar to him. It took me four goes to finally pass my driving test, and indeed, after the third test, my examiner said, "I'm not really allowed to tell you this, but don't come back to test in a manual car again." Uncle Tony told me a wonderful story about how Dad was learning to drive, panicked, and tried to drive his Dad's brand new Austin the wrong way round the roundabout. I've been called obsessive about my passion for music. Uncle Steven told me about my Dad having a similar passion as a child for football, and how he used to give pretend football commentaries as a way of sending his brothers to sleep. We even had the same attitude towards suits. I never saw the importance of wearing a suit to my university interview either, so the thought of his Dad going to the lengths he did to find the perfect suit for him, only to find that the interviewer couldn't see, seems about par for the course.

Peter was a loving husband and father, and his wife certainly feels privileged to have spent so many happy years with him. We may believe he has left this Earth prematurely, but in truth, that's not how he would want us to remember this day. He would want us to talk about the fact that he led a full life, and how he achieved everything he wanted to achieve at each point in his life. He wanted to retire to Lanzarote in a couple of years' time, and if we can summon up the courage, we'll take him there, but for now his spirit will be around to guide us, in much the same way he did when he was alive, and if he is watching over us, and listening to this now, I hope he knows that I couldn't be more proud to have been his son.

The many messages of condolence we received from people that he had known over the years gave a clear picture as to how well- liked and respected he was, and gave us some comfort in our hour of need. We have compiled a memorial book with all the letters inside, and we love to look at this as it gives us a gentle reminder of our very special husband and father.

Chapter 25

Our New Home

The day before Peter's funeral, I had started looking for places to rent, as I recognised that it would be difficult for my parents and us to live together for any length of time as there wasn't room, and we were all very independent and different generations. I felt Christopher playing his music, which was very much an acquired taste, would be a little too much for them. I found an apartment to rent in a converted mill in Summerseat, Bury, at a reasonable rent, and arranged to move out of my parents' home once the furniture, which was in storage in Essex, had arrived. I was taking notice of what you are always told: that after a bereavement you shouldn't make major changes for at least a year. I reasoned that after I had rented for six months, I would then be in a position to know whether I wanted to return to Essex, but it would be so different without Peter, and I felt that there would possibly be too many memories.

I and Christopher moved into the apartment, and Christopher proceeded to apply for work. The difficulty we had was that his qualifications were in the languages of Japanese and Chinese, but he didn't have anything relating to business, and jobs with these qualifications were very thin on the ground. What followed was a succession of temporary jobs, but nothing permanent was on the horizon. This was a very difficult time for both of us, and at this point I don't feel I coped as well as I could have done. Mum's solution, if I was depressed, was "Have a glass of wine", but I quickly realised that this wasn't the answer. I tried to motivate Christopher in his search for work, but finally he decided that the solution was to work abroad again, so a matter of months after coming home Christopher was moving once more. I was now faced with not only losing Peter, but Christopher too. However, I did recognise that this might be the only solution to Christopher's job hunting. He obtained a position in South Korea teaching English as a foreign language, which thankfully he was qualified in. However, I was determined I wouldn't lose Christopher as well, so during the next couple of years I travelled to South Korea to visit him, which is no mean feat for a woman alone.

My first trip to South Korea was a very nerve-wracking experience for me. I didn't speak the language, and wasn't sure how much English was spoken. On the flight out I was sat next to a young South Korean woman who was studying in the UK, and going home to visit her family. She told me that when I arrived I would have to catch a train to the bus terminus, and which platform I needed. I don't think I would have managed without her assistance.

Christopher was based in a place called Jeonju, and I was to travel by coach, which was a four-hour journey. At the end of the flight I was really quite jet-lagged, but I managed to board the correct coach; and, thankfully, Christopher was waiting for me at the coach point. The reason why the coach took so long was that they kept stopping at service stations for people to get off and buy food. I didn't alight as I was worried the coach would go without me, and I wouldn't be able to find my way.

After meeting Christopher, he told me that he would take me to his apartment to drop off my bags, and then his school had booked a meal for us. I was so tired, but it was so nice that they had taken the trouble to welcome me. The teachers were a mixture of Australian and American, and they had booked a meal at a local restaurant and taken the trouble to make sure they served western food too. I was told that I was the first parent to have visited, and they were very happy to see me. After the meal, they booked a karaoke room, which is the norm in South Korea; a group hires a room and stays all night if they want to. I managed a few hours, but then I really needed to sleep. I slept for two days solid.

Christopher and I had a few days holiday booked, and we visited Seoraksan; yet again, a long coach journey, and we stayed at the Kensington Star, so named because when we arrived, we discovered that there was an old London bus in the garden, and throughout the hotel there were pictures of Prince Charles and Diana. This was their version of a themed hotel, and was quite bizarre. The hotel was situated in the Seoraksan National Park, and our room had a view of Seoraksan Mountain, which is the highest mountain in the Taebaek Mountain range. The Seoraksan National Park has been designated a Biosphere Preservation District by UNESCO. We had many walks through the Park, and there were many rare species of plants and animals. I really enjoyed my stay with Christopher, but the stay was far too short.

Chapter 26

Insurance Predicament and Ghani's Reappearance

I still had yet more hurdles to go through when I arrived back, as I had to find a solicitor so that we could sort our financial affairs, which was a little more difficult as Peter had had his own consultancy business—but, thankfully, I found a lovely one called Anne, who helped me through all the difficulties. One of the problems we came up against was that we had a life insurance policy for Peter, but the insurers were dragging their feet on making settlement. I was still so distraught about everything that had happened that I wanted to just forget it. However, Anne persuaded me that it was a genuine claim and we must fight it, as if we didn't it could happen to someone else. At one point they wanted Peter's passport as they thought he was alive, and I was going to meet him in another country. As you can imagine, this was very upsetting for me. We later found out that a man had taken a boat out and faked drowning, and then his wife had picked up the proceeds and met him abroad. After learning of this I fully understood why I was having difficulties, and actually had some sympathy with the insurance company. I understand that the man must have been in tremendous debt, but if anyone else decides to take this route, I would urge them to think of how it might affect other people.

I settled in my apartment which was in a converted mill, and felt that I probably wouldn't hear anything further from Sudan, but I received an email and a telephone call from Ghani. He was now based in London, working at his profession as a journalist, and wanted to come and see me to make sure that I was okay. I really appreciated this communication since at this point I was wondering what I would do with the rest of my life. The fact that someone cared what happened made an immense difference.

He told me that he wished to come and visit me, and bring his wife and two little girls. As I was living in an apartment with no garden, and a barbecue seemed a good idea, I asked Mum and Dad if the meeting could be at their home. When they arrived, there wasn't just Ghani's family, but his wife's sister. Each of them had gifts of flowers for us. Mum said she felt like the Queen. The family had travelled down from London to see us, which I greatly appreciated. That afternoon we took them for a walk in the Burrs Country Park, and they exclaimed at the green of the countryside in comparison to the desert in Sudan. I talked to Ghani at length, and he said he appreciated that I wouldn't be going back to Sudan, but wondered if I would be prepared to continue with helping them to learn English in Sudan. I said I would be happy to do this, but I couldn't envisage ever going back without Peter. Unfortunately, this didn't come to pass.

I have heard from Ghani from time to time since and I would love to see him again, but I don't know whether this will happen. I will always feel that I left an extended family in Sudan. To me it will always be that we achieved a lot, but, because of circumstances, were unable to finish the job.

He also told me that one of Peter's students, who Peter was very fond of, had tried to find me to make sure that I was okay. This particular student gave Christopher some American dollars as we were leaving Sudan, and told him to give it to me when we were on the plane as I would be too proud to accept his help. I will forever be grateful to the people in Sudan who assisted me at a time of great need.

At this point, a special mention should also go to Yasir, my manager, who stayed with me for the last days, travelling with me in the van to obtain the necessary paperwork so that I could get Peter home. At one point, Mohammed asked Yasir to get out of the van, and let him take over, and I said that under no circumstances did I want Yasir to leave. Yasir stayed, and this took a lot of courage as he was very frightened of Mohammed, who was also his boss.

Chapter 27

Back to My Roots

It took a while to sort the financial affairs, but once this was settled I decided that I didn't want to return to the family home in Essex as there were just too many memories. A larger apartment came up for sale in the converted mill I was living in, and I felt I was getting older, and this would be a secure environment for me, so I bought it. It did need some work doing on it; mainly, a new kitchen as it was pretty basic. The person I employed to carry out the work was a cowboy builder although very plausible. He took the deposit off me, and then pretended to be carrying out the work. He told me that he had almost finished, and could he have an advance on the final sum as there had been a few more jobs to carry out? I think at this point I was gullible, as I paid out the money and he just left shortly after, not finishing the job. Despite numerous telephone calls and the promise of completion, it never happened. To take him to a small claims court would have caused lots of stress, and then I probably would only have got a settlement of a few pounds a week. I decided to write this off as experience, and learn from it.

Thankfully, friends we had before our life in Africa rallied round and supported me otherwise I don't know what I would have done. Gillian, who I had been close to while we were teenagers, and was a bridesmaid at my and Peter's wedding, helped me to move into the apartment, and when I had the problem with the cowboy builder she enlisted her brother, who was a kitchen fitter, to help me. Another contact of Gillian's, Michael, assisted me with fitting a new boiler. As the apartment was a listed building, we were limited as to what we could fit, and in fact Michael helped a lot when I needed little jobs doing. Whilst I was living there, I sometimes felt that the corridor smelt musty, but thought it was because it was an old building. Not the case! One day I arrived back from shopping, and the police were in the corridor. The apartment opposite had been raided, as they were growing cannabis in it. I had noticed many people coming and going from it, but just thought the tenant was very popular.

Sometimes the grief would overtake me for no apparent reason, and I would just find myself welling up. I found I was often in conversation with Peter; I asked him what to do, or sometimes I would feel quite angry at him for leaving us. So many emotions go through your head at this time. After Christopher left to work in South Korea, I felt so alone as all my family had left now. The nights were the worst as when it is quiet, it is a time when you can think. I found that most evenings I was having a glass or two of wine, but I soon realised that this wasn't the answer. I had to pick myself up and be strong. I can understand, however, how people turn to drink after the bereavement of a loved one. I spent my days walking, and evenings meeting friends and socialising

Chapter 28

My Greek Adventure

I thought about it at length, and decided I needed to put my life together, and I booked a holiday in Greece. I had never been away alone, as for most of my adult life I had been part of a couple and then a family. I decided to be brave and go for a month, as I felt that this would give me much needed time to recover. I went on a group holiday so that I wouldn't be totally alone, but I found many people were in couples, and didn't know whether it was my choice to be alone. I felt very alone as all I really wanted was Peter back, but I was determined to make a go of my new life since I could have many years alone now. However, I made many new friends on this trip, as I was determined not to be miserable as this was a holiday; and I took each day at a time, and each one became a little easier. I would never forget Peter, but I was learning that life goes on.

When I arrived back from Greece, I decided that I would treat Mum to a holiday as she had been so good when we came back. I discussed it with her, and she had always wanted to go to Switzerland so I booked a holiday for us near to the mountains. I hadn't been away with Mum for thirty years so I didn't know how we would get on.

We arrived in the middle of an electric storm, and we had a short train journey after the flight, which was a little scary, and then we got in the lift at Lausanne, which we shouldn't have done, and it was stuck between floors because of the storm; but we eventually arrived at the hotel we had booked, but we were quite late. There was no one on the desk, and all we had was a short note saying that our room was on the second floor. I couldn't work the lights so we staggered to the room, and just fell into bed. I remember saying, "Hopefully it will be better tomorrow."

The following morning we woke up to bright sunshine. This was an adventure for Mum as she had been the same as myself, always going away with family. We walked out of the hotel and caught the underground to Lake Geneva where we purchased tickets for the boat. What we didn't find out until our last day was that we had been sitting in the first-class seats. We thought it was a little unusual that underneath us people were packed like sardines. We enjoyed it there as we ordered bread and wine, and had a lovely view of the Alps. The captain came up to us at the end of the day, and told us we were sat in the wrong place. I said, "It doesn't matter; I will pay the difference." I think he was a little embarrassed to ask so he charged me the equivalent of £1. Mum couldn't believe my cheek. We couldn't stop laughing.

Another place we found was a very expensive restaurant, which we loved, and we became very friendly with the owner, who introduced us to an English couple who were born very near to where we lived in the UK. The couple invited us to dinner, and we were amazed at their home; it was like a stately home in England, with a swimming pool and a nuclear bunker in their basement, which was fully stocked with wine, but we didn't see any food. We were both a little tipsy when we climbed in the taxi to take us back to the hotel, and Mum had got it into her head that our hosts had something to do with arms smuggling. It was just her imagination going wild, but this holiday I really connected with Mum, and we had a lot of fun.

I did go on holiday with Mum and Dad at a later date to Gran Canarias, and we had a lot of fun as Dad was a ballroom dancer and

I had learnt to dance at a young age so I could partner him. I will always remember the holidays I had with my parents, particularly now as both Mum and Dad have passed away. Both were diagnosed with different cancers, and unfortunately it was terminal. I spent a lot of time with both of them when they were ill, and still miss them. However, both their and Peter's memorials are at the same crematorium so I get to visit them and take flowers

Mum and Dad died the same year, but thankfully, just before Dad died all the family went on holiday to celebrate their golden wedding. Mum received a telegram from the Queen which she was very proud of.

My life is very different now as I have married Kevin, and when he retired we decided to live where we wanted to, and we now live in a village which is very close to the borders of Lancashire, Yorkshire, and the Lake District. We have travelled to many countries, including New Zealand, Canada, and South America. Kevin said that my life had been in two parts: my time with Peter, and now with him, and I still wear both Peter's and Kevin's rings. The one valuable lesson I have learnt from everything that has happened is to never put off till tomorrow what you can do today as tomorrow may never come

Christopher has now studied for an MA in English as a Foreign Language, and is working as a lecturer at a university in the North of England. He lives very close to me, and I can see him regularly. I feel Peter would be very pleased with what has happened, but he would probably say, "What took you so long?"

Conclusion

This story takes place before Sudan was split into two countries, Sudan and South Sudan. At the time I lived there, they had just brokered a peace agreement, which they hoped would be successful so it was relatively stable at this point. The oil refinery was in Sudan, but the oil was in what is now South Sudan. I listen to the news now, and I am very sad about the troubles that are happening there.

I would be considered an old person now, and probably wouldn't be suitable for establishing a language school, but Sudan will always remain in my heart, and a part of me will always be there. I hope that the situation will improve, but I think that unless they stop fighting between themselves, this will never be the case. I remember I was on a flight back to England sat next to a man from the UN, and he told me that if they got their act together they could feed the whole of Africa. I have no doubt this could be achieved.

I may not be in Sudan, but I am very conscious that they need assistance to develop, and with this in mind I support charities that are giving assistance by way of practical aid. The three charities I support are the Red Cross, Practical Action and Water Aid, but of course there are many more based in Africa.

Sudan, for myself, was the most massive learning curve, and I am so proud of what we managed to achieve. I know if Peter was still here he would feel the same despite the consequences for him and the family.

This book is about my experience, and how I saw it, being a western woman.